DEFENCE OF ARMAGEDDON,

OR

OUR GREAT COUNTRY FORETOLD IN THE HOLY SCRIPTURES.

IN TWO DISCOURSES.

DELIVERED

IN THE CAPITOL OF THE UNITED STATES, AT THE REQUEST OF SEVERAL MEMBERS OF CONGRESS, ON THE ANNIVERSARY OF WASHINGTON'S BIRTHDAY, 1857.

BY F. E. PITTS,

OF NASHVILLE, TENN.

"Thou hast magnified thy word above all thy name."
Ps. cxxxviii, 2.

Doomed by an edict written in the sky,
The monarchies of earth shall be no more:
Heaven's sealed wonders open to the eye
In rising glories on the western shore.

TENTH EDITION.

BALTIMORE:
PUBLISHED BY J. W. BULL,
PROPRIETOR OF COPY-RIGHT.
1862.

Sherwood & Co., Prs.

TO THE AMERICAN PUBLIC.

The theory of Armageddon, by the Rev. F. E. Pitts, has been in course of preparation for years. Immense research and mental labor have brought it into being. For nearly two years it has been before the public and met the favorable notice of many of the ablest journals and reviews in America. Learned theologians, civilians and statesmen have freely accredited its truthfulness, and mathematicians pronounce its chronological argument *demonstration*. Indeed, almost all who examine it believe it. The exceptions to this rule are generally found amongst the subjects of the British Crown, or those who imagine that England, *par excellence*, is the model of the nations.

Having learned that Armageddon leaves the autocracy of Britain in the whirlpool too, they have become offended, and of course denounce it.

Mr. Pitts believing most firmly the principles and positions of the theory to be true, and that a correct appreciation of the subject is of untold interest to the American people, he has, from motives sincerely patriotic and pious, discussed the claims of this sublime theory before thousands of our countrymen in various portions of the United States.

Mr. Pitts certainly deserves the highest praise of his countrymen. Modest and unassuming, though a giant in intellect, and richly stored with the treasures of science, he has brought out a work that must elevate and encourage our noble confederacy more effectually than any book that has appeared since the birth of the Republic.

The work has now passed into the fourth edition, and will, we have no doubt, soon be issued by the hundred thousand. This book should be in the hands of every American citizen, because of the advance that it will give to true patriotism, and the enthusiasm that it has and necessarily will create for the Union.

NOTICE.

FROM THE NATIONAL INTELLIGENCER,

February 24, 1857.

SERVICES AT THE CAPITOL.—In place of the Rev. Mr. Waldo, Chaplain of the House, Rev. F. E. Pitts, of Nashville, Tennessee, appeared agreeably to previous announcement, and delivered a discourse on the fulfillment of prophecy, with reference to the United States. With no leaning to cant or fanaticism, and with no tendencies to a politico-religious sermon, the reverened speaker entered upon his task of unfolding the prophecies, both of the Old and New Testaments. The events which he detailed with reference to our own country, were made to fit with such surprising chronological accuracy to the predictions, that it was by the almost unanimous desire of a large and attentive audience that his lecture was continued in the afternoon. At the appointed time, three o'clock, P. M., it was no easy task to find a seat in the great hall of the Capitol, so deeply interested were the people to hear the sequel of the morning discourse, a brief outline of which we are herewith enabled to present to our readers:

HIS introduction to the investigation indicated with what reverence and discretion any attempted elucidation of the meaning of prophecy should be conducted; that the prophecies touching the nations, down to the fall of Jerusalem, were but a literal history of Syria, Edom, Moab, Egypt, and Judea; but from the destruction of the Jewish capital down to a certain period called "the time of the end," a vail was on the prophets, and no interpretation of the sublime visions during that interdicted age could possibly be correct; for God had repeated the announcement to Daniel, the prophet, that "the words were closed up, and the vision was sealed till the time of the end." That this was not the end of the world was evident, for in the time of the end "many should run to and fro, and knowledge be increased;" that then "the wise should understand, but the wicked should not understand." Not only was the vision itself sealed, but the time or end of these wonders, and especially the theatre of these wonders, or the land of their realization, should be unknown till God was prepared for their accomplishment. That "the time of the end"—an age of great intellectual energy, adventure and locomotion—was the age in which a great nationality would arise; that the United States arose at the end of 1290 symbolic days from the destruction of Jerusalem; that Daniel's 70 weeks being equal to 603 years and 129 days of solar time, according to the eclipses of the sun, gave an infallible rule to determine symbolic time; so that if 70 symbolic weeks eqnaled 600 years and 129 days, 1290 symbolic days reached from the burning of the temple on the 189th day of the year 68, A. D., to the 4th of July, 1776; and that, making the starting-point at the occasion of the daily sacrifice. which happened, according to astronomy, at sunrise, three minutes past five o'clock, A. M., on the day the temple was burnt, the 1290 days run out at a quarter to three o'clock, P. M., on the 4th day of July, 1776; and, from the best sources of information, the Declaration of Independence was proclaimed at that hour on the glorious Fourth. That the United States was the fifth Government represented by the stone cut out of the mountain without hands. The image ef Nebuchadnezzar represented the successive kingdoms of Assyria, Medo-Persia, Macedonia, and Rome; that the iron and clay in the feet and toes of the image, symbolized the union of Church and State under Constantine, June 19, A. D. 325; that the antagonism of the stone to the image smiting it on the feet, symbolized the genius of our great nation in its opposition to the union of Church and State; that while the stone-kingdom, or government, *were not* Christianity, the mountain out of which the stone was cut *was* Christianity. That the winged woman of the wilderness was an emblem of Christianity, and her man-child, to whom was given "a rod to rule," was an emblem of our government, arising from a pure religion; that this man-child, being "caught up to heaven in the clouds," showed the providential protection of our infant Republic. That our nation, answering the moral portrait of the nationality which was to come, was Israel restored. That God would constitute such a nationality out of a people who would acknowledge his Son Jesus Christ, and not of the Jews, who, from the beginning, have denounced Christ. That perfect coincidence being perfect fulfillment, our nation and no other on earth answered the picture. That the nationality to arise was to be gathered out of the nations. That they were to go westward That the country they were to inhabit was a land between the eastern and the great western seas. That the land was one "that had always been waste." That it was to be located in *thirteen* distinct States. That these States should be bounded on the east by the eastern sea, and on the west by the great western sea. That the people gathered out of the nations should "build and dwell safely in unwalled villages and cities, having neither gates nor bars;" "a land of broad rivers and streams;" a Republic where the people "should appoint to themselves one head," and their rulers and governors "should be from among themselves." That the United States was "the isles that should wait" for God, and that the ships of Tarshish or Old Spain should be first to open emigration. That our country was "the land shadowing with wings" which was beyond the rivers of Ethiopia, which, from Judea beyond the Nile, was the United States, and no other country. That our great country was divinely protected in its beginning, and, answering the predictions precisely of the nationality that was to come, is the "nation born to God in a day"—born on Independence Day. That the United States arose in the providence of God, as the model political government; and that its great mission was the overthrow of monarchy, and the utter destruction of political and ecclesiastical despotism.

His subject in the afternoon related more especially to "the last great battle between civil and religious liberty on the one hand, and political and ecclesiastical despotism on the other, termed in Scripture the "Battle of Gog and Magog;" the battle of "Armageddon," and the battle of the "great day of God Almighty." That the United States would be invaded by monarchy. That Russia would be the leading power, and England, and all the autocracy of the world, would be allied with Russia against the United States, except France; that France would be with us in the end as she was with us in the beginning. That an armament such as the world never saw, composed of millions, would invade our country. That the battle-field was the valley of the Mississippi. (See Ezekiel xxxix, 11.) That Heaven would be upon our side. But in this last dreadful fray there would be trouble such as never was. That the United States, being the exponent and representative of Republicanism, extending its borders from sea to sea, and from the lakes to the gulf, arose as the formidable defiance of autocracy; and that Russia, embracing an area of one-seventh of the earth's terra-firma, and arising in dreadful grandeur must, in self-defence, attempt the extinction of popular freedom; and that these two formidable powers, lowering and culminating to the heavens like dreadful clouds surcharged with the elements of ruin, would shock the world with their collision and drench the earth with blood. That our great country would *never be divided.* That our Union, like a noble ship, though her live-oak timbers would bend and quiver in the tempest, would ride the storm in safety. That monarchy would be overthrown for ever, and Republicanism every where prevail, and nations learn war no more. Then sets in that millennial day, when science, commerce, manufactures and the arts would spread, the religion of the Son of God have sway, "righteousness and peace among the people walk, Messiah reign, and earth keep jubilee a thousand years."

But an imperfect sketch of these lectures is here presented. They certainly created a profound sensation. True or false, the clearness and conclusiveness of the arguments, as presented by the intelligent speaker, we think it would be difficult to answer. Surely, the theme is startling and sublime. The appropriate allusion of the speaker to the portraits of Washington and Lafayette that hung on the walls in the Capitol, in his allusion to France being with America in the final struggle, was deeply affecting

THE UNITED STATES OF AMERICA

FORETOLD IN THE HOLY SCRIPTURES.

In entering the sublime arcana of inspired prophecy, we are deeply impressed with a scene that is laid in the land of Midian, where, from the burning-bush, the voice of Almighty God arrested the attention of the wondering prophet: "Put off thy shoes from off thy feet; for the place whereon thou standest is holy ground."

No subject presented to the human mind imposes profounder reverence, greater caution, and deeper research, than an elucidation of prophetic truth; and yet no theme has been more prolific of fanaticism among the incautious and adventurous in almost every age.

We must look to the Scriptures themselves for direction to a true and legitimate interpretation of their own meaning. It is important also to discriminate between "secret things that belong to God, and things that are revealed, which belong to us and to our children." For want of this discernment, Millerism, and all that class of fanatical fancies, have deluded misguided thousands. Whenever, therefore, an interpreter of prophecy attempts to tell when the day of judgment will come, just rest assured he is wise above what is written; for we are taught by the Great Prophet himself, "Of that day, and hour, knoweth no man; no, not the angels of heaven, but my Father only." This Divine announcement should always quiet such unauthorized pretensions.

It must be universally conceded that the Almighty has interdicted a knowledge of some sublime subjects, which he alone will fully reveal and explain by their own accomplishment. Notwithstanding, it is equally evident that there are certain portions of prophetic truth that he himself designed should be understood by the sons of men, for it is written, "Blessed is he that readeth and they that hear the words of this prophecy." Here, then, is a Divine encouragement to study inspired prophecy. But how can we be beneficiaries of this promise, though we may both read and hear, if, at the same time, we cannot understand them?

A few self-evident propositions we will now submit, as indispensable principles for the investigation of prophecy—principles that must form the only true and infallible *criteria* to determine their intended meaning.

First. All prophecy is either *plain* and *literal*, or *obscure* and *symbolical.*

Second. A plain and literal prophecy may be understood prior to fulfillment, just as well as subsequent to the event predicted. For example, Jesus Christ said, "There shall not be left here one stone upon another that shall not be thrown down." His meaning was too obvious to be misunderstood.

Third. But an obscure or symbolic prophecy cannot possibly be fully known, however impressive the general outline of the subject; yet the special application of the prediction to time, event, and circumstances cannot be understood until fulfillment settles the true meaning. There may be several interpretations of an obscure prophecy offered *a priori*, provided they be legitimate; that is, if such definitions are not unreasonable or incompatible with the nature of the subject. Nevertheless, we must bide our time till fulfillment determines the meaning intended. As an example, it is written, "Behold, I will send you Elijah the prophet before the coming of the great and dreadful day of the Lord." Now, it is evident that one legitimate interpretation of this prophecy was the same entertained by the Jews, that God would send the old prophet in person, for it expressly states, "Elijah the prophet." But it so happened that another man altogether, John the Baptist, coming "in the spirit and power of Elias," is said by Christ to be "the Elias which was for to come."

Fourth. A perfect coincidence of character, circumstances, and events with any given prophecy, is perfect fulfillment. This is so plain and patent that we cannot deny it without denying the very proof of the Messiahship of the Son of God. When John sent his disciples to Christ to inquire, "Art thou he that should come, or do we look for another?" "Jesus answered and said unto them, Go and show John again those things which ye do hear and see: the blind receive their sight, and the lame walk, and the lepers are cleansed, and the deaf hear, the dead are raised up, and the poor have the gospel preached unto them." As much as if he had said, John will have sense enough to know that in whomsoever these coincidences are found, he is the Messiah.

With these principles to guide us, we proceed to the investigation of our subject

The United States of America, our great country, is foretold in the Holy Scriptures.

We are fully apprised that the novelty and sublimity of our subject, upon its bare announcement, will awaken the incredulity of some, and enlist the opposition of others. To all such we politely bespeak the courtesy of a candid hearing. We are not concerned that you receive or reject the truth of this theory, but we *are concerned* that you carefully examine the testimony upon which it rests. Do you believe the Holy Scriptures? "Then hear me for my cause."

But that you may understand that we do not attempt to prove what is unreasonable and absurd, we propose the following question:

Is it at all probable that our great country, with its teeming magnificence, now the fear and glory of all lands, *would have been overlooked by prophecy?* How comes it to pass that smaller countries, and lesser kingdoms, retired hamlets, solitary islands, and seaport towns; that Edom, Moab, Egypt, and Syria; that Tarshish, Tyre, and Sidon, with the rest, are particularly programmed upon the inspired page, and our land the only portion of God's *terra-firma* that is proscribed a place in the book—that prophetic book that professes to map the world till the end of time? Has the inspired penman no account, no place for a nation that is at this very moment telling more upon the intellectual and moral destiny of the world than any other under heaven? Do you believe it? And yet you must believe it if our theory is a fable.

The possibility of the truthfulness of our subject is certainly deeply interesting; the probability of the fact is startling; but the clear and unanswerable demonstration of that truth is actually sublime.

The predictions of the Bible touching the nations, down to the destruction of the Jewish capital, are indeed but a literal history of Egypt, Moab, Syria, Edom, and Judea. Here all is plain and self-evident, as time has witnessed the fulfillment. But from that memorable event, the downfall of Jerusalem, on to a certain chronological period, called by Daniel "*the time of the end,*" all is obscurity. No interpretation breaks the seal of its wonders. Clouds curtain the heavens; and the symbols that glow in the vision of God's holy prophets are alike mysterious to them and to the wondering seraphim.

To Daniel, the prince of the prophets, this great truth seemed first to have been announced. When the prophet had the stupendous visions covering that symbolic period, he exclaimed: "I heard, but I understood not: then said I, O my Lord, what shall be the end of these wonders? And he said, Go thy way, Daniel; *for the words are closed up and sealed till the time of the end.*" This positive declaration of Jehovah was thrice repeated to the prophet. But Gabriel gives him to understand personally thus much: These wonders will not occur in your day, Daniel; you will rest with your fathers long before the seal shall be broken; nevertheless, you will arise in the resurrection of the just; therefore, go thy way, and be comforted with the blessed hope. Such we suppose to be the meaning of the angel, when, closing his sublime mission to the prophet, he said, "But go thou thy way till the end be: for thou shalt rest, and stand in thy lot in the end of the days."

That *the time of the end* was a certain chronological length, and not the end of the world, is very certain, for things are said of *the time of the end* not at all consistent with the scriptural account of the day of judgment. In the time of the end "many should run to and fro, and knowledge be increased;" then "the wise should understand, but none of the wicked should understand." Whereas, in the final day, we suppose the wise and the wicked will both understand. These expressions evidently characterize that period called the time of the end, as an age of great locomotion, intelligence, and enterprise. And the words "wise" and "wicked," being generic terms, and nouns of multitude, doubtless refer to nations. The friends of civil and religious liberty shall understand, but subjects of absolutism, and the dupes of despotism, shall not understand.

As the visions of Daniel, that covered the lapse of ages to *the time of the end*, were sealed and closed up, it is conclusive that the visions of Isaiah and Ezekiel, Jeremiah and John, embracing the same subjects and measuring the same period, are interdicted also. This is a legitimate and necessary deduction.

Now, is it not very surprising that eminent men, deeply pious and profoundly learned, have never discovered the "*seal*" of the Divine interdiction placed upon these visions? The impenetrable mystery, by Divine authority, hangs before their eyes, while the vague and unsatisfactory explanations of the most gifted commentators confirm the truth of the Divine prohibition. The truth is, there is not one writer in the long learned catalogue of commentators on the prophecies, down to our present theory, but has attempted to explain the meaning of these symbols by principles and rules that were known and applied during the interdicted ages, and are consequently necessarily erroneous; for God had again and again declared, "*the vision is sealed, and the words are closed up till the time of the end.*"

Two obvious truths are here revealed: 1. The closing up of the vision down to a certain period. 2. As the sealing of the vision was only *till* that time, of course when that time should come the seal would be broken and the vision be understood.

If, therefore, the period when these sublime disclosures should be made was to be characterized as an age of vast enterprise, intellectual energy, and moral adventure; and if we live in such an age—an age marked with unparalleled progress and discovery—we ask, with the profoundest reverence, may we not venture to inquire, and to inquire hopefully, for the meaning of these wonders?

Should it be demanded, why have not the erudite and the learned in ages past apprehended this interpretation of prophecy, we have already anticipated the inquiry: that God had sealed a knowledge of these wonders during those ages. But should the unassuming pretensions of the learned author of Armageddon be looked upon as a barrier to a candid investigation of this most deeply interesting theory, we have only to suggest that great and ingenuous minds are too magnanimous for such uncandid evasion. As the gifted author himself has asked, "May not a child find a gem?" Was it not a poor peon of the mountains that first discovered the riches of Peru? But perhaps one material reason why our great country has hitherto never been dreamed of as the burden of prophetic truth, has been owing to the fact that most of the principal writers on prophecy have been Englishmen, who, putting one foot of the compasses down on Great Britain as the centre of creation, and describing a circle, have invariably left out the United States of America; somewhat after the fashion of a Chinese map of the world, which, after giving to the Celestial Empire almost the entire map, puts down Europe and America on a space no larger than a penny, calling them the "Barbarian Islands."

We will certainly be excused for disposing of another class of captious cavilers. It has been asked with much emphasis, "What good, or what purpose, could the truth of such a theory accomplish?" This inquiry, we will apprise you, is never made by the learned or the considerate; certainly not by one who reveres the truth of the Holy Scriptures.

What is the design of prophecy? Surely, wise and glorious accomplishments were intended by the Almighty in communicating to his servants the words and visions of prophecy. Doubtless, to inspire the hope of man for their realization, and to confirm the faith of mortals in the divinity of those truths by their fulfillment. But where will you find a broader field for such accomplishments, or a more glorious theatre for the fulfillment of prophetic truth, than in the providential rise and prosperity of a great nation that should be the exponent and example of popular freedom—a nation whose principles and progress should excite the admiration and arouse the emulation of the whole earth? Let men but behold, on this magnificent scale, a fulfillment of those sublime symbols and announcements that have staggered the philosophy of men, and baffled their profoundest learning from age to age; then indeed infidelity would seek annihilation for shelter, and its last refuge of lies be swept from the face of the earth.

We shall first consider the *symbolic predictions* of the United States.

THE TIME OF ITS RISE.

The rise of a great nationality is evidently predicted by Daniel, when "the power of the holy people," or friends of civil and religious liberty, shall *cease to be scattered;* when the wise nations should understand, and "many should run to and fro, and knowledge be increased." This glorious era was to be the period called "the time of the end." The rise of the United States of America synchronizes with that "time," and no other nation under heaven.

The chronological argument is purely mathematical, and we believe unanswerable.

The decree of Cyrus for the emancipation of Israel was published in the last month of the year 537 B. C., (about December 6th,) as is found by the coincidence of an eclipse of the sun, predicted by Thales the Milesian, that occurred B. C. 601, as well as the historic account of those ages. The crucifixion of Christ was on the 25th of March, A. D. 29, (*Vulgar era,*) as found also by an eclipse of the moon and historic records. And the destruction of the Jewish state began on the 21st of Nisan, A. D. 68. The 70 weeks of Daniel were to begin at the decree of Cyrus, and to end at both the other named epochs. From the decree of Cyrus to the crucifixion, was 564 years and 109 days; and from the same decree to the last general Jewish passover, was 603 years and 129 days. These two lengths were embraced in the 70 weeks, and show the precise duration of those weeks, as exactly those many years and days transpired to reach the events predicted. This fact no one can deny. Now the explanation of the matter is simple: the 70 weeks are Hebrew weeks of years, or 490 years. But these are *abbreviated weeks;* that is, they require the addition of one or more kinds of sacred time to complete them. By adding the sabbatic days which would be in 490 years, we have 560 years. These are symbolic years of 360 parts; and as a symbolic year may stand for any Hebrew year of years, it may stand for the one of 364. Then we have the equation of time, as 360 : 364=560 : $566\frac{2}{9}$.

These $566\frac{2}{9}$ years are composed of 364 days each; and by reducing them to solar time of 365 days, 5 hours, 48 minutes, and $47\frac{1}{10}$ seconds to the year, we have 564 years and 109 days, as the fulfillment exhibits.

In a similar manner the other results will be found; but this example is a sufficient illustration of the principle of explaining sacred time.

3

The $3\frac{1}{2}$ times of Daniel, chapter xii, are, by this mode of explanation, easily understood. Three and a half times, or years, are equal to 1260 symbolic years. To this, if we add sabbatic years proportionably, we have 1440 years; and again adding proportionable sabbatic years, or one to every six, we have 1680 years. Then, as the symbolic year of 360 parts may represent any Hebrew year, it may represent the year 366 days or parts. We then have the following equation:

$360: 366 \times 1680 = 1708$ years, or 623,833 days, 17 hours, 1 minute, and 40 seconds.

These $3\frac{1}{2}$ times were to begin at the *cessation of the daily sacrifice*. The daily sacrifice was offered at sunrise. The sun arose at the meridian of Old Jerusalem on the 189th day of the year 68, A. D., about 5 o'clock, A. M. This, then, is the beginning of the $3\frac{1}{2}$ times, or the 1260 symbolic days, or the 2300 "evening mornings." An "evening morning" was a lamb sacrifice at sunrise, and a lamb sacrifice at sunset—two lambs to a day; so 2300 are equal to 1150 days; add the proportion of sabbatic time, and 2300 evening mornings equal $3\frac{1}{2}$ times. These lengths all agree, and embrace, in solar time, 623,833 days and 17 hours; and, from the last Jewish sacrifice, end, at the meridian of

Philadelphia, at a quarter to three o'clock in the afternoon of July the 4th, 1776.

Another length of these times is 1335 days, which, by the same rule, equal 1810 solar years, and will end in 1878. These two endings begin and close "*the time of the end*," and answer to the rise of the American Republic and the expansion into the millennium. The 1290 and 1335 days coincide with the two lengths of the 3½ times.

In brief, Daniel's 70 symbolic weeks embrace the time from the decree of Cyrus to build and restore the city and temple, to the crucifixion of Christ and the final destruction of Jerusalem, which, in solar time, was 564 years to the first event and 603 years to the latter. And from this last event, the destruction of the holy place, it was to be 3½ times, or 623,833 days and 17 hours, to the rise of a great nationality.

Now, if 70 symbolic weeks are equal to 564 solar years, 3½ times, or 1260 symbolic days, are equal to 1708 solar years; but 1708 solar years, or 623,833 days, reach from the burning of the temple on the 189th day of the year 68, A. D., to the 4th day of July, 1776.

Let it be remembered, the 70 weeks call for two endings—the cutting off of Messiah, and the destruction of the holy place. But these two events are 39 years apart. The two lengths are made out legitimately by adding the proper sabbatic time of days, weeks and years, as authorized by the Jewish calendar; for the weeks themselves are "*determined*," *nectag*, *cut short* or *abbreviated* weeks. So that both lengths are accurately fulfilled, and are correctly termed "70 weeks."

But to suppose, as do most all of the old commentators, that a day means a year, and that 70 weeks are to be understood as 490 years, is to fall short of the events predicted, 94 years in the first case, and 113 years in the second; consequently, their theory is false. But time has not only demonstrated the error in their opinion of the 70 weeks, but also their error in relation to the 1260 and 1290 days that were to follow. If days meant years, pray tell us what great nationality arose at the end of 1290 years after the destruction of Jerusalem? or what other great event happened that could possibly be construed into a fulfillment? Positively none.

The calculation, being purely mathematical, and guided by astronomy, has been rigidly made to the tenth fraction of a second, and must be reliable. The interpretation of the chronology is legitimate, for it is governed by Daniel's 70 weeks; consequently, the fulfillment is shown in the rise of a glorious civil and religious republic exactly at the end of these symbolic lengths, and that republic is the United States of America.

The fifth government in the dream of Nebuchadnezzar, or the stone kingdom, symbolizes our great nationality.

The king of Babylon saw in his vision a vast image, "whose brightness was excellent, and the form thereof was terrible. This image's head was of fine gold, his breast and his arms of silver, his belly and his thighs of brass, his legs of iron, his feet part of iron and part of clay." In this terrific image, as interpreted by the prophet, God showed to the Assyrian monarch the whole of monarchy to the end of time, in four great dynasties that should consecutively arise, his being the first of the series: "Thou art this head of gold. After thee shall arise another kingdom inferior to thee," etc. It is universally admitted by the learned, that the Assyrian, the Medo-Persian, the Macedonian, and the Roman empires, are clearly and unequivocally represented here, and that, too, in the order in which they arose. In the fourth or iron portion of this image, another substance enters into the formation of its feet and toes, of which a more minute and extended description and interpretation are given than of any other part of the dream: "And whereas thou sawest the feet and toes, part of potters' clay, and part of iron, the kingdom shall be divided; and there shall be in it of the strength of the iron, forasmuch as thou sawest the iron mixed with the miry clay. And as the toes of the feet were part of iron, and part of clay, so the kingdom shall be partly strong, and partly broken. And whereas thou sawest iron mixed with miry clay, *they shall mingle themselves with the seed of men;* but they shall not cleave one to another, even as iron is not mixed with clay." That the two materials constituting the feet and toes should always have been understood to represent a division of the kingdom into a stronger and weaker part of the civil government, is the only opinion perhaps ever offered by commentators in every age. The theory of Armageddon alone maintains that the division of the fourth empire, as represented by the feet and toes, symbolizes the ten kingdoms, which, according to Bishop Newton, was the exact number that actually did arise from the old Roman empire; but that the *iron* and *clay* in the feet and toes symbolized the *union of Church and State,* and nothing else. With this interpretation the words of the angel perfectly agree, and are impressively intelligible: "Whereas thou sawest iron mixed with miry clay, *they shall mingle themselves with the seed of men; but they shall not cleave one to another*, even as iron is not mixed with clay." That is, as a perfect chemical amalgam with the two cannot be formed, because the ingredients will not cohere, so the union of Church and State will never be happy in its combination—never a harmonious and peaceful union—but an illegitimate commerce, unsanctioned by the will of God, and ruinous to the best interests of the human family. "They shall mingle themselves with the seed of men." That is, a superior order of men will join an inferior order; or the Church shall be joined to the State, and, consequently, such a government must always be partly strong and partly broken—a politico-ecclesiastical concubinage that would curse the nations of the earth.

This interpretation is greatly strengthened by the chronological character of the image; the iron and clay enter into the composition of the feet and toes, after that the Roman empire for a thousand years had stood upon its iron legs, a nation of soldiers. The date of the feet synchronizes most wonderfully with the event represented; for Church and State union in the Roman empire began under Constantine, A. D. 325, and was perpetuated with each of the ten-toe kingdoms that swarmed out of the old Roman hive.

Such was the image and its legitimate interpretation, a knowledge of which is essential to a correct understanding of the fifth or stone kingdom.

"Thou sawest till that a stone was cut out without hands, which smote the image upon his feet that were of iron and clay, and brake them to pieces. Then was the iron, the clay, the brass, the silver, and the gold, broken to pieces together, and became like the chaff of the summer threshing-floors; and the wind carried them away, that no place was found for them; and the stone that smote the image became a great mountain, and filled the whole earth." Of this sublime symbol the angel gives the following interpretation: "In the days of these kings shall the God of heaven set up a kingdom, which shall never be destroyed; and the kingdom shall not be left to other people, but it shall break in pieces and consume all these kingdoms, and it shall stand for ever. Forasmuch as thou sawest that the stone was cut out of the mountain without hands, and that it brake in pieces the iron, the brass, the clay, the silver, and the gold; the great God hath made known to the king what shall come to pass hereafter; and the dream is certain, and the interpretation thereof sure." Let it be observed, the word kingdom, in the prophecies, is a convertible term with government, and must be so understood in this passage.

The absurdity of applying the stone kingdom to Christianity is so very obvious, it is indeed remarkable that the learned should endorse such an opinion. The stone could not symbolize Christianity, 1. Because it did not arise at the *proper time* for Christianity. "*In the days of these kings*" must refer to that plurality of kings last mentioned, the ten-toe kings or kingdoms, that arose from the Roman empire. The philosophy of our language demands this sense. But Christianity arose in the days of one king, Augustus Cæsar. In point of fact, then, the truth of history for ever forbids any other interpretation. Our great nationality arose exactly in the days of that very plurality of kings or kingdoms that came out of the old Roman dynasty. 2. The stone kingdom did not arise in the *proper place* for Christianity. Rome arose where the Grecian empire had stood, the Grecian or Macedonian succeeded Medo-Persia, and Medo-Persia was successor to the Babylonian or Assyrian kingdom; but the stone kingdom had no previous connection with this corporate image of monarchy; did not grow up under its shadow, precincts, or presence, but comes from a distance, and strikes the image from *without*, and, at one dreadful stroke of *external* violence, breaks the colossal image to fragments; and its atoms, ground to infinitesimal dust, fly like chaff before "the winds of the summer threshing-floors." But Christianity arose within the dominions of Rome: Judea was a Roman province where Christianity was born. 3. The stone kingdom could not have arisen at all at the time that Christianity arose, or it would have arisen in the Roman empire also; for Rome at that time embraced the known world. At the birth of Christ, "There went out a decree from Cæsar Augustus, that all the world should be taxed." But there was a land, my countrymen, where the Roman cohorts were never marshaled—a land that Heaven had concealed from the cupidity and ambition of her conquering armies. That land is our own beloved America, the only portion of the globe, beyond the limits of ancient Rome, where a great nationality, in its constitution, character, and mission, could possibly answer the true meaning of the fifth symbolic kingdom that the God of heaven would set up.

As the political governments of monarchy were severally represented by a symbol taken from the mineral kingdom in one corporate connection, showing the uniformity of the genius that pervaded the whole, so the fifth government, being political also, is symbolized by a mineral type (a stone) likewise. But being entirely distinct from and unconnected with the image of monarchy, it is very clear that the fifth government is not only a political organization, but an anti-monarchical government; consequently, a political republican government, arising under the supervision of Almighty God "a stone cut out of the mountain *without hands:*" brought into being and glorious nationality by a wonderful chain of Divine providences.

The violent destruction of the monarchical image by the stone, necessarily implies political organization and military power. The mild and tranquil genius of Christianity offers no violence to any man, or any nation; but it wins its gradual conquests by moral suasion. But here is a power dreadful as the enginery of battle, swift and destructive as the bolt of heaven. And did Christianity indeed break down and annihilate the Roman empire? What a failure! Was it not the barbarian hordes of Goths and Vandals from the North that overran imperial Rome? But how are we to account for the stone smiting the image "*on the feet?*" Why was the attack not made upon the head, or upon some vital part? Let it be remembered, the *feet* was the point of the union of Church and State; consequently, the mission of this great fifth nationality was the destruction of State and Church union, as well as the utter and ultimate extermination of ecclesiastical and political despotism from the face of the earth. Now, we appeal to the assembled wisdom before us, to profound statesmen, and venerable ministers of God, if the antagonism of the stone to the iron and clay is not fully answered in the genius of the American people? Are not the sentiment and feeling of this great nation more harmonious and universal in their hostility to Church and State union than on any other subject? Has not the Constitution of the United States, in devoting a whole chapter to the subject, raised an eternal barrier against it? And is not our nation the only enlightened government among the nations of the earth, where the illegitimate union of Church and State is most solemnly interdicted? thus leading our free people to "Render unto Cæsar the things which are Cæsar's, and unto God the things that are God's."

While it is, therefore, conclusive that the stone kingdom is a providential political government, "cut out of the mountain without hands," incompatible with, hostile to, and destined in its great mission to annihilate the last vestige of monarchy from the nations of the earth, it is equally evident that "the mountain" out of which the stone is cut *is Christianity*. So our great government is founded upon the Bible. Remove this indestructible basis that supports the fair fabric of our political institutions, and we have no government. The Declaration of American Independence evidently recognizes the obligations of the *first*, and fully embraces the principles of the *second* great commandment. The smiles of a Christian Sabbath inspire the devotion, and call from labor to rest our toiling millions; while the obligation of every officer of state, from the chief magistrate of the nation down to the humblest minister of justice, is rendered inviolate by a solemn averment upon Divine revelation.

The history of the world confirms the fact, that a nation's religion moulds the character of its civic government. A despotic, superstitious, and bloodthirsty system of religion will form and fashion its

4

political economy after the same model. So a pure, enlightened, and divinely authorized religion has ever been the maternal source of a pure, liberal, and happy civil government.

As, therefore, the four great empires were to be succeeded by a fifth great government, altogether differing in its principles and character, and as the United States of America is the only great nation that ever has or ever can arise to answer the description and fill the mission of that fifth empire, the conclusion is inevitable, that our glorious republic is the stone kingdom that the God of heaven was to "set up."

A glimpse of this sublime reality inspired the good Bishop Berkeley, more than a hundred years ago, to declare what even now seems a wonderful consummation:

> "Westward the star of empire makes its way;
> The first four acts already passed,
> The fifth shall close the drama with the day:
> Time's noblest offspring is the last."

The United States of America is symbolized by the man-child of the winged woman of the wilderness. "And there appeared a great wonder in heaven: a woman clothed with the sun, and the moon under her feet, and upon her head a crown of twelve stars.

And there appeared another wonder in heaven ; and behold a great red dragon, having seven heads and ten horns, and seven crowns upon his heads. . . And the dragon stood before the woman which was ready to be delivered, for to devour her child as soon as it was born. And she brought forth a man-child, who was to rule all nations with a rod of iron ; and her child was caught up to God, and to his throne. . . And to the woman were given two wings of a great eagle, that she might fly into the wilderness, into her place. . . And the serpent cast out of his mouth water as a flood, that he might cause her to be carried away of the flood. And the earth helped the woman, and the earth opened her mouth, and swallowed up the flood which the dragon cast out of his mouth. And the dragon was wroth with the woman," etc.

It is almost universally admitted that the true Church of God is represented by the woman in this symbol. And, without pausing to examine the many opinions which divines have entertained as to the true meaning of the man-child—some supposing it refers to Christ, and others to Constantine—we will demonstrate that the symbolic meaning of the man-child is that of a great nationality that was to arise under the superintending providence of Almighty God in the latter times; and that that great nationality is the United States of America.

To this man-child a *rod* was given to *rule*—always the ensign of political power; so that, while the mother represents a pure, enlightened religion, her offspring, "a man-child," who is invested with political authority, must represent an enlightened nationality. This exposition we claim with great confidence to be legitimate. We shall now show that such is the testimony of the Holy Scriptures. Isaiah declares, "Before she travailed, she brought forth; before her pain came, she was delivered of a *man-child*. Who hath heard such things? who hath seen such things? Shall the earth be made to bring forth in one day? or shall *a nation be born at once?* for as soon as Zion travailed, she brought forth." In this passage, the term "*Zion*," meaning the Church of God, settles, beyond all doubt, the symbolic meaning of the "*woman* clothed with the sun;" and as the "man-child" in the one case is put in apposition with "*a nation born at once*," he must be understood in the other instance to be the symbol of *a nation* also. We cannot deny the explanation without denying the interpretation the Holy Scriptures give of their own symbols.

But is this nationality, arising from a true and

enlightened religion, the United States of America? We shall see. In the first place, the man-child was the offspring of a true and enlightened religion. 2. Its destruction was determined upon, in its infancy, by a great red dragon. 3. It received "a rod," in its infancy, to rule, or to maintain political jurisdiction. 4. He and his mother were favored by the "earth." 5. "The child was caught up to the throne of God."

Now, how remarkably does our great nation answer to this description? Our nationality arose from and was the legitimate offspring of an enlightened liberal religion. Our honored ancestry, having fled from the storms of persecution in the old world, sought to find in the new, freedom to worship God; the founders and framers of our political fabric being, in the main, worshipers of the true God, and believers in his Son Jesus Christ. Our infancy was warily watched by the demon of despotism, and fearful were the efforts made by the dragon of autocracy to crush us in the cradle. But "the earth helped the woman." The seat of the old Roman empire is termed, in the symbolic language of the Apocalypse, "the earth." And did not several of the European powers come to our assistance in that dreadful conflict? Russia declared neutrality, Spain, and especially Holland, waged war against England, while the fleets of France came to our rescue in our Revolutionary struggle. "The earth helped the woman," and the man-child was rescued.

But we were specially protected and defended by the providence of Almighty God, which we understand the expression, "caught up to the throne of God," to imply. How wonderful the eventful history of our new-born nation! Who can trace the special interventions of a Divine hand through all the stages of our infant existence, from our natal hour, without acknowledging that the God of Washington was on our side?

The coincidences are so numerous, and the agreement of our great nationality with the symbolic description of the man-child so wonderfully accurate, that the conclusion is demonstration. For if perfect coincidence be perpect fulfillment, then the United States of America is symbolized by the man-child of the winged woman in the wilderness.

The United States of America is the nationality that is promised in the prophetic Scriptures to arise in the latter times as *Israel Restored*. It has long been a favorite theory, both with Jewish and Christian writers, that the nationality to be gathered together in the latter days, was understood to mean the returned or restoration of the scattered sons of Abraham to the land of Palestine. We are not surprised at the confidence with which this opinion has been entertained from age to age, because it is a legitimate *a priori* interpretation, seeing this nationality is called "Israel" by the prophets. In a conversation had with a venerable Bishop of the Episcopal Church, he inquired of us: "Sir, by what construction of language do you make the great nationality, promised to arise in the latter times, to mean the United States? That the Bible authorizes us to expect such a nationality there can be no doubt; but how do you make out that nationality to be the United States of America, as it was promised to be *Israel?*" To which we replied: "Beloved Bishop, the predictions of the prophets are put up in Hebrew dress; the regalia is Mosaic, the custom is Israelitish. They did not say, friends of civil and religious liberty, Americans, or even Christians; but they used the best terms they had on hand: they said '*Israel.*'"

Only doff the subject of its Jewish robes, and the symmetrical proportions and sublimity of Christian republicanism are as perfectly delineated as a Grecian pillar. But we will now show that what is reasonable and legitimate is a true principle of interpretation, being authorized by the great Teacher from heaven. Said the disciples to our Lord, "Why say the scribes that Elias must first come?" for it is written, "Behold, I will send Elijah the prophet, before that great and notable day of the Lord." "Jesus answered and said unto them, Elias is come already, and they knew him not, but have done unto him whatsoever they listed. Then the disciples understood that he spake unto them of *John the Baptist.*" Now, suppose the difficulty of the pious Bishop were proposed to our Lord: "Master, by what construction of language do you make out that John the Baptist, the son of Zacharias and Elizabeth, is indeed Elias the prophet, which was for to come, seeing he is in reality another man altogether?" Does not the same difficulty exist in both cases; and has not our Lord, by answering the objection in the one case, removed it in the other? John was "the Elias which was for to come;" not because that was the name by which he was called in his generation among men, but because he came "in the spirit and power of Elias," thereby answering the moral portrait that was drawn by the pencil of inspiration, and was, consequently, declared by the

Saviour to be indeed the Elias. If, therefore, a great nationality is promised to arise in the latter days, and the United States of America exhibits the character of such nationality, as delineated by the pen of prophecy, arising "in the spirit and power" of Israel to come, and no other nation under heaven ever has or ever can answer the description, then, perfect coincidence being perfect fulfillment, our glorious republic is the nationality which was to be gathered together in the latter times under the prophetic name of Israel.

Let it be remembered, that the term Israel was a cognomen of honor, and not the natural right of a Jew. God gave the appellation to Jacob, because "as a prince he prevailed with God." While the children of Jacob maintained their integrity, they enjoyed this high distinction; but St. Paul defends the application of the term to Gentiles who may possess the proper claims to this honor.

But perhaps the most plausible bill of exceptions taken to our theory is presented here. It is suggested, with much apparent reason, that we are too wicked and unworthy a people to bear the honored title of Israel. Alas for us, my countrymen! Heaven knows full well that we are wicked enough; for when we consider the special providence of Almighty God, marvelously exercised over us from the very infancy of our organization, through every change of fortune—what prosperity has crowned our cause—how we have been guided and guarded by a Divine supervision, as virtually present as the *holy Shekinah*, "in a cloud by day, and a pillar of fire by night"—and then look at the abominations that pollute our national escutcheon, it is humiliating in the extreme. Look at the blasphemy that outrages the highest obligation of created beings, marring the purest language on earth, in desecrating the name of the holiest Being in the universe. Look at the violation of even heathen honesty, discrediting character in almost all gradations of society. See the frenzy of political parties, disrupting the very bonds of brotherhood; while blood and debauchery infect the air and pollute the earth, bribery, homicide, and murder transpire in the very halls of our nation's councils.

But bad as we are, fellow-citizens, we are the very best people upon the face of the earth. The great heart of our magnanimous country beats responsive to the sighs and sorrows of all nations. Our peaceful land is the hospitable home for the oppressed of all countries. Our laws are the transcript of eternal justice. True, we have neither titled dukes nor hereditary lords, but the emoluments of profit and honor are offered to the deserving of all classes, and our loftiest promotions are accessible to the humblest poor. Though denounced abroad by an aristocracy that dooms its own pauper millions to proscription, beggary, and starvation, yet our institutions, which they fain would pity, are the pulsations of health, compared with the plague-spots of pestilential Europe.

Already have three hundred thousand of our African population become the Christianized children of God—a greater number of true Christian converts, heathens as their fathers were who first came amongst us, than are to be found in all the missions of all denominations upon the earth. We have colonized a happy republic also, upon the benighted shores of their fatherland. Our ministers of mercy have gone to every heathen shore, and preached glad tidings to almost every island that dots the bosom of the ocean. Beams of light, radiating from this central home of civil and religious liberty, already break upon the distant millions that weep in the shadow of death.

When the noble Greek is crushed by the hoof of Turkish despotism, the halls of our Senate are eloquent with a sympathy that responds in the bosom of a whole people. When Poland, Hungary, and Italy struggle and fall, the hope of the American people struggles and falls with them. When the cry of starvation is heard from ill-fated Ireland, American transports are freighted with the munificent offering of a generous people. And, moved by a magnanimity which knows no parallel, our swift ships are dispatched to recover England's lost navigators in the regions of eternal snow.

We have the one living and true God, one Saviour, and one religion—one Constitution, one Confederacy, one Republic, one nationality; therefore, a true religion and a true civil government is the Israel that was to come, the "nation born at once"—born on the 4th of July, 1766.

But let us not be misled by the consecrated name of Israel. For "all are not Israel who are called Israel." A nation possessing the true religion, and enjoying an enlightened and liberal civil government, may have many unbelieving and rebellious people in its midst; and, doubtless, millennial glory, and the day of judgment also, will find both the righteous and the wicked, the just and the unjust, the wise and the foolish virgins, for the wheat and tares will grow together until the general harvest, "which is the end of the world." Even Israel restored to nationality will not be the Eden of bliss.

It was in the brightest days of the Hebrew nation when the tribes of Jacob were led out to the solitudes of the desert to behold the glory of God revealed upon the sacred mountain. Clouds of awful grandeur encircled its brow. Lightnings rent the mantle of the sky, and deep-toned thunders rocked Mount Sinai from its glowing summit to its granite base. Then, where was Israel—God's own Israel? Behold him at the foot of the hill making a *golden calf!*

By the term Israel, therefore, we mean to be understood, a providential nation, possessing the only true religion, and a divinely sanctioned form of civil government. Such, with all its sunshine and shadows, was ancient Israel, and such is the United States of America, and the United States of America alone.

As to the scattered Jews—who have long since lost all genealogical proof of their respective tribes—forming such great nationality any where, that is supremely ridiculous. That they may return to Jewry, we think highly probable; because every thing formerly connected with that nation was typical. Their fiftieth, or Jubal year, was a time when the scattered Jews returned to their respective homes, and were put in possession or seized of their patrimonial estates. This custom may anticipate the jubilee of the world; that is, when republicanism shall become world-wide. Then the Jews, in masses, may return to Canaan; for the Almighty by deed of gift made Abraham and his posterity proprietors of that land. They may return and form a little Christian republic in Palestine. But to become the great national headship of the world, restore temple-worship and priestly offerings, with all the gorgeous paraphernalia of its ancient sacerdotal splendor, is but the pious dream of fanaticism. The simplicity and spirituality of the religion of the Son of God forbids the idea; while the burdensome rites of the Jewish ritual have long since been discarded by the unostentatious loveliness and grace of a Christianity that claims to worship the Father "in spirit and in truth."

But even the supposition that they will return and form a literal government in their ancient home may be a mistake. For those prophecies that seem to refer to their literal restoration are interpreted by many worthy divines to foretell their conversion to their long-rejected Saviour. This is indeed plausible.

> "In foreign climes they'll cease to roam;
> Nor, weeping, think on Jordan's flood;
> In every land they'll find a home,
> In every temple worship God."

And so mote it be. But if the Almighty designed to honor a people by raising them to become a great nationality, of whom is it probable such nationality would be composed? Let this question be settled by a plain principle of Divine revelation. Who are the Jews? A persecuted and disbanded people. Why are they persecuted? For rejecting the claims of the Son of God. From his very birth to this day they have, as a nation, derided and discarded him. They sealed the dreadful imprecation at his crucifixion: "His blood be on us, and on our children." But there is another persecuted people—the friends of civil and religious liberty. They have been hunted down in every land, like the hart of the mountains. They have been proscribed and execrated, outraged and banished, in every age; and, for conscience' sake, have been martyred by the million. Why were they persecuted, "scattered, and peeled?" For accepting and acknowledging Jesus Christ. Here, then, is the difference. Now, apply an infallible principle which must test this question. Said the adorable Saviour, "If any man serve me, him will my Father honor." Is it, then, at all probable that God would honor a people by the promised glorious nationality, who have, as a nation, spurned the mercy of the Prince of peace, and obstinately persisted, before the eyes of all nations, in rejecting the clearest evidence of his Messiahship, during the long, long night of their wanderings; and yet, at the same time, pass by a people who, through every change of fortune, propitious and adverse, have firmly maintained their faith in Christ, and invincibly breasted the storms of persecuting vengeance for his glorious name's sake? Will heaven honor a people who dishonor his Son, and overlook a people who were ready to live and labor and suffer and die in his blessed cause? The case being self-evident, and the rule to determine our judgment infallible, the decision must be inevitable.

Christianity mourns the ill-fated children of a divinely chosen and illustrious ancestry, and ardently prays for their conversion to Christ. But even this glorious consummation our faith beholds far in the distance. That the Jews will ultimately embrace Christianity, we entertain no doubt; but they will be the last nation on the face of the earth that will be converted. For "the blindness that has happened to Israel" will remain "until the fullness of the Gentiles is brought in." That is, the Gentile world will be converted to God before the blindness of infidelity will be removed from Israel. To suppose the conversion of the Jewish nation to be the means of converting the Gentile world, is, consequently, directly opposed by the words of the apostle. In their case we behold the verification of another gospel maxim: "The first shall be last, and the last first." They were the first to hear the blessed tidings of man's redemption from the lips of its glorious Author, "but they received him not." And the Apostle Paul, in his valedictory to his own countrymen, declares, "Seeing that ye judge yourselves unworthy of eternal life, lo, we turn to the Gentiles." So, also, the melting strains that mingled with the tears of the Son of God over their devoted city announced the same calamity. "O Jerusalem, Jerusalem, thou that killest the prophets, and stonest them which are sent unto thee; how often would I have gathered thy children together even as a hen gathereth her chickens under her wing, and ye would not. . . If thou hadst known, even thou, the things which

5*

belong unto thy peace, at least in this thy day, but now are they hid from thine eyes. . . Henceforth is your house left unto you desolate; for I say unto you, he shall not see me henceforth till ye shall say, "Blessed is he that cometh in the name of the Lord." That is, Ye shall see me no more until you will be rejoiced to hail me as your Messiah. This is, doubtless, its true meaning.

There are very many passages of Scripture which are universally admitted by the learned and judicious to foretell the rise of a great nationality in the latter times. These predictions cannot, by any reasonable construction, be applied to the rise of such nationality in the land of Judea; but are most wonderfully descriptive of the United States of America, and of no other country under heaven.

We shall now select a few out of the many marked descriptions and coincidences only realized in our favored land and nation.

First. The land of the promised nationality was to be located *between two seas*—the eastern sea and the great western sea: "From the border unto the east sea, this is the east side. . . The west side also shall be the great sea; from the border, this is the west side." Ezek. xlvii, 18, 20. These broad boundaries of our great country are perfect; the west side being the "great sea," is most remarkable. Judea is not bounded on the east side by a sea at all. This passage, which is taken from the prophet's geographical description of the land of restored Israel, cannot possibly apply to Palestine, if Ezekiel has given its true boudaries. All commentators understand this chapter as an inspired account that maps the country of the promised nationality ; but it is absolutely impossible to locate this land in Palestine, for the want of an eastern border. No sea bounds old Canaan on the east. Learned men have generally supposed that Palestine is the country referred to, but let learned men show us that eastern boundary. This defect is fatal, and must for ever vitiate the claim of Judea to this high distinction.

Second. This land is described as being hitherto uncultivated and unimproved—a land "that has always been waste." Ezek. xxxviii. Of course Palestine cannot be referred to here, for it cannot be said in truth that Judea has always been waste. But our own country fully answers the description. Our primeval prairies and grand old woods presented, on the arrival of our ancestors, the same unbroken wilderness they had remained for ages, as though Heaven had specially preserved them for the glory of their future destiny. Let it not be said that the footprints of the aborigines of this country are an objection to this account; for that land is waste where tillage has never harvested its blessings for man. But such is the desert description of the country to be possessed by the nationality to come, and such was the new continent of America.

The song of the eloquent Isaiah can remind you of no other country: "The wilderness and the solitary place shall be glad for them; and the desert shall rejoice, and blossom as the rose. It shall blossom abundantly, even with joy and singing: the glory of Lebanon shall be given unto it, the excellency of Carmel and Sharon, they shall see the glory of the Lord and the excellency of our God. . . For in the wilderness shall waters break out, and streams in the desert. And the parched ground shall become a pool, and the thirsty land springs of water: in the habitation of dragons, where each lay, shall be grass with reeds and rushes."

Third. That wonderful country was to be inhabited by a people "gathered out of the nations." Ezek. xxxviii. Not of one nation collected together that had been scattered amongst other nations, but, what is obviously the sense of the passage, composed of people of different nations. This is so prominent a character of the glorious nationality to come, that the prophets seem to dwell upon it with rapture and inspired eloquence. "Lift up thine eyes round about, and see: all they gather themselves together, they come to thee: thy sons shall come from far, and thy daughters be nursed by thy side. Then thou shalt see, and flow together, and thy heart shall fear, and be enlarged; for the abundance of the sea shall be converted (turned) unto thee, the forces of the Gentiles shall come unto thee. . . Who are these that fly as a cloud, and as doves to their windows?"

The prophet enriches his sublime description by images drawn both from the animal and the vegetable kingdom: "The multitude of camels shall cover thee, the dromedaries of Midian and Ephah; all they from Sheba shall come. . . All the flocks of Kedar shall be gathered together unto thee. . . The glory of Lebanon shall come unto thee, the fir tree, the pine tree, and the box together." Isa. lx. As if the holy seer had said, Emigration shall come from the land where the dromedaries roam; they shall come from the land where the fir tree blooms. "Therefore thy gates shall be open continually: they shall not be shut day nor night."

Did ever such a tide of emigration set into any country since the creation of the world as continually swarms to our hospitable shores? Indeed, the citizens of these States, or their fathers, have come from almost every country under heaven. But the prophet enters into detail: "Strangers shall stand and feed your flocks, and the sons of the alien shall be your ploughmen and your vine-dressers. . . And the sons of strangers shall build your walls, and their kings shall minister unto thee." Now, the walls of a country's defence are its public improvements; and it is notorious that the sons of strangers build most of our public works.

"The sons also of them that afflicted thee shall come bending unto thee; and all they that despised thee shall bow themselves down at the soles of thy feet." The sons of the very soldiery that invaded your coasts, murdered your people, and burnt your towns and villages, should come to make your country their home; and those who sneered at your experiment of popular freedom, attempted to crush it in the cradle, predicted the downfall of American Independence, and that liberty would die with Washington, and with his dust receive the same rites of sepulture—yes, even they should come and seek a refuge and a home in your happy land. How imposing the picture drawn by the pencil of inspiration here; and how wonderfully true is the fulfillment!

Fourth. In the promised nationality, unlike the political economy of ancient Israel, foreigners were to be allowed a place to dwell, enjoy their homes and the pursuits of happiness, in common with the citizens of the country; but it seems from the prophet, the rights of suffrage and eligibility to office were only to be enjoyed by those strangers who had lived long enough in the land to raise their native-born children: "And it shall come to pass, that ye shall divide it by lot for an inheritance unto you, and to the strangers that sojourn among you, which shall beget children among you; and they shall be unto you as born in the country among the children of Israel; they shall have inheritance with you among the tribes of Israel.— And in what tribe the stranger sojourneth, there shall ye give him his inheritance, saith the Lord God." Ezek. xlvii, 22, 23. There could be no propriety in characterizing that class of foreigners who should be blessed with children born in the land, from the stranger who is only a sojourner, whose residence is but recent and transient, unless peculiar privileges were understood to belong to the fathers of native-born children. As we lay no claims to the politician, we will be allowed strongly to approve of this interesting feature in the economy of restored Israel. Our land should always be the welcome home of foreigners; but, at the same time, they should remain long enough to appreciate our blessings, learn our laws, and the genius of our wonderful constitution, before they aspire to dictate or to govern.

Fifth. The principle of *extension*, in enlarging the boundaries of their primary possessions should specially characterize the prosperity of the promised nationality.

"Lift up thine eyes round about, and behold: all these gather themselves together, and come to thee. . . For thy waste and desolate places shall even now be too narrow, by reason of the inhabitants, and they that swallowed thee up (the autocracy of the Old World) shall be far away, (beyond the sea.) The children which thou shalt have, (in this land,) after thou hast lost the other, (ancient Israel,) shall say again in thy ears, The place is too strait for me: give place to me that I may dwell." Isa. xlix, 18, 20,

Extension seems to be the genius of our free institutions. From thirteen States, we have already multiplied into thirty-one, besides nine territories that soon will be ready to enter into the Union.

We need give ourselves no uneasiness about Mexico, Cuba, and Central America. Monarchy and anarchy must melt away in the immediate proximity of a glorious republic; while the natural interests of those countries will impel them to seek annexation, that they may also enjoy in common with us the benign blessings of our happy confederacy. Indeed, the words of prophecy, legitimately interpreted, warrant that the domain of this nationality will embrace the entire continent of North and South America. For its "dominion shall be from sea to sea, and from the river unto the ends of the earth." We know this passage is usually applied to Christ, to which we make no objection. But will you restrict it to him? If so, you greatly diminish the universal triumphs of his reign. We are taught that his sway shall be illimitable, and every knee shall bow and pay homage to him. But the passage before us is a clear territorial grant, issued by Divine authority, and must mark the boundaries of Israel that was to come. The geographical description can be found applicable to no other country but ours. Here the grant finds all of its metes and bounds. "From

6

sea to sea:" from the Atlantic to the Pacific Ocean. "And from the river:" the Mississippi, the father of waters, with its sixty thousand miles of tributary navigation, and the incalculable tonnage of its transports. "Unto the ends of the earth:" to the most remote promontories in the North, and to Terra del Fuego and Cape Horn in the South. We must be excused from dwelling further on the emigration that was to come to this land. These predictions are very numerous and wonderfully accurate—inspired predictions, that never have been realized, and never can be, unless they are fulfilled in the New World. We will, however, notice one other.

"Behold, these shall come from far; and, lo, these from the North and from the West; and these from the land of Sinim." Isa. xlix, 12. Now, all commentators agree that "Sinim" is China. The fact is, it was its true ancient name: *Thinim*, *Thina*, or *China*. It is so put down in the ancient maps. And China lies "north" and "west," or north-west of us. In the message of Ex-Governor Bigler, of California, some two years ago, it is there published that there were then some sixty thousand Chinese in that State. Now, no commentator questions that this passage describes emigration coming to the land of restored Israel, for the whole context confirms it. But how are the Chinese to come from China to Palestine and come from the *north-west?* It is impossible. Here is a promise made of emigration from a distant country, whose inhabitants have never been known to mingle with other nations; here their true ancient name is given; here is the very direction which they were to come; and here is a fulfillment upon a most magnificent scale. Perfect coincidence being perfect fulfillment, our position is demonstration.

Sixth. The land of restored Israel is described as a country *restored from its desolations, by the peculiar construction of its towns and villages, and the prosperity and quietude of its inhabitants.*

In the invasion of this land, at the last great battle, by Russia and the autocracy of the Old World, the prophet thus addresses the power that leads that invasion; "After many days thou shalt be visited: thou shalt come into the land that is gathered out of many people, against the mountains of Israel, which have been always waste; but it is brought out of the nations, and they shall dwell safely all of them. . . Thou shalt say, I will go up to the land of unwalled villages; I will go to them that are at rest, that dwell safely, all of them dwelling without walls, and having neither bars nor gates. To take a spoil, and to take a prey; to turn thy hand upon the desolate places that are now inhabited, and upon the people that are gathered out of the nations; which have gotten cattle and goods, that dwell in the midst of the land." Ezek. xxxviii, 8, 11, 12.

Here, my countrymen, is almost a daguerreotype portraiture of your own land. We very much question whether Ezekiel the prophet ever saw an "unwalled" city in his life. Surely, if old Palestine is to be brought back again to her more than ancient splendor, "unwalled" cities and villages will not be found there. This passage, therefore, can never be applied to Judea; for all her cities were walled, from Jericho to Jerusalem. This remarkable description of the numerous villages and cities, and the possessions, prosperity, and security of the people, is a grand and graphic delineation of the United States of America, and of no other country on earth.

Seventh. The infancy of that country should receive the attention of royal patronage: "Kings shall be thy nursing fathers, and queens thy nursing mothers." How very remarkably this has been realized will occur to the mind at once. The term "nursing" applies to infancy. And it was in the early history of our people that the supervision of royalty was exercised over us. The names of several of the old thirteen States, besides many counties and towns, still perpetuate the recollection of royalty: Georgia and Virginia, Maryland and the Carolinas, as well as King and Queen and King William counties, Prince George, Prince Edward, and prince we don't know what else—names that will for ever perpetuate the fulfillment of prophecy in what might otherwise seem to be only accidental.

Eighth. A country remarkable for the *number of its majestic rivers.*

"But there the glorious Lord will be unto us a place of broad rivers and streams; wherein shall go no galley with oars, neither shall gallant ship pass thereby." Isa. xxxiii, 21. This passage from the prophet is admitted to refer alone to the land of restored Israel. But if that land be Palestine, how are we to see the force of its meaning? Can the river Jordan and the rivulet Kedron answer the grandeur of this description? Certainly not. But the many mighty and majestic rivers in our own country fill up the prophetic map upon a sublime and magnificent scale. By the expression, "there the glorious Lord will be unto us a place of," etc., we understand that he will guarantee that description of country to the nation he would raise up. "Wherein shall go no galley with oars," is very singular. The Hebrew word, translated "galley," literally signifies *a government clipper*, sent out by a superior kingdom to exact port-dues from a dependent people. The loss of the tea-cargo in Boston harbor fully illustrates this subject; while the very genius of our independence, in the days of Andrew Jackson, was stamped upon a medal: "*Millions for defence, but not one cent for tribute.*"

Ninth. The land of restored Israel is described to be literally *more elevated* than any portion of the world.

"The mountain of the Lord's house shall be established upon the tops of the mountains, and all nations shall flow to it." The willful king of the North says in his proclamation of war against us: "I will *go up* to the land of unwalled villages." Lieutenant Maury has shown, in one of his late learned works, that the United States of America is the highest part of the visible earth, and that it is down stream from the ports of our country to every other continent and island of the globe. But if this elevation must be morally and intellectually understood, and not literally, still, the realization being as perfect in the one case as in the other, our argument remains conclusive.

Tenth. The *peaceful character of the inhabitants, and the intelligibility and uniformity of their language*, should designate that people.

"Thou shalt not see a fierce people, of a deeper speech than thou canst perceive; of a stammering tongue, that thou canst not understand." Isa. xxxiii.

Polite manners and gentle deportment every where characterize the American people: this is a world-wide acknowledgment, so that the solitary exceptions are gloated over by the detracting prints of roving authors as morsels too precious to be erased from their journals. But the uniformity and intelligibility of our language is indeed most extraordinary. Although teeming thousands are constantly pouring into our communities from the Germanic States, France, and other countries, our pure vernacular Anglo-Saxon will conduct you safely through any portion of our vast domain. And it is now contended, by those competent to judge, that the English language is more correctly spoken in the wilds of America than at the court of St. James—

more accurately pronounced in our primary schools than in the British Parliament. We do not question their intelligence nor their energy, but Americans speak the English language better than the English themselves. Should the pride of an Albion tempt him to deny it, just put him upon his trial with any word where the consonant *h* is to be supplied or omitted—the monosyllable *hell*, for instance—and if he be not satisfied with an attempt to spell and pronounce it, you may give him up as incorrigible.

Eleventh. The rapid advancement of *intelligence* and *divine instruction* should mark the rising progress of that people.

"Many shall run to and fro, and knowledge be increased." "All thy children shall be taught of the Lord, and great shall be the peace of thy children." What nation presents such a spectacle at this very moment as the United States? Our literary institutions are scattered all over the land, so that the humblest poor may be enriched with the treasures of science; while millions of sheets in the republic of letters pour floods of light upon the human mind. Here the press is free, that mighty enginery of thought, guarding the majesty of law and the inviolable sanctity of the Constitution. Here the pulpit, unawed by the terrors of the throne or the thunders of the Vatican, in tones of power and tongues of flame, proclaims "the acceptable year of the Lord," and preaches glad tidings to the poor. Here the word of God is an unchained book; and, like the sun in mid-heaven, rifts the clouds that mantle the world, shedding a strong and steady light upon the shadowy mansions of the dead, inspiring the living with the ecstatic hope that our loved and our lost shall awake from their dusty beds in the last glorious morning.

Twelfth. The country inhabited by the people "gathered out of the nations" should be settled in *thirteen distinct States*, like as it was with Israel; only "Joseph should have two portions."

"Ye shall inherit the land according to the twelve tribes of Israel: Joseph shall have two portions." Ezek. xlvii, 13. It is a remarkable fact that although the Jews had but twelve tribes, the portion falling to Ephraim and Manasseh, children of Joseph, being divided, made them a confederacy of thirteen states or tribes. It is also just as remarkable, that in the beginning we had but twelve States; and William Penn held the charter of Pennsylvania for twenty years before he obtained that of Delaware, and then we had thirteen States also. But the coincidence in the boundaries of the thirteen states of restored Israel with those of the old thirteen United States, is still more remarkable. The prophet gives the eastern border of each tribe to be the *eastern sea*, and the western border of each tribe to be the *great western sea*. (See Ezek. xlvii.) Wilson, and perhaps Bancroft, affirm, that the original charters of the thirteen United States called for the Atlantic or eastern ocean for their eastern boundary, and the Pacific or the great western ocean for their western boundary, in almost so many words.

It is not a little amusing to see the perplexity of the great and good Dr. Clarke, in attempting to map the land of restored Israel. He lays his plot, of course, in the territory of old Palestine. He bounds his thirteen lots by the Mediterranean or western ocean, but, for the life of the learned Doctor, he can find no *eastern sea* for his eastern border. The little Dead Sea lies across three of the tribes, but does not bound any one of them! Examine his map, at the close of his commentary on Ezekiel, and you will find, for want of an eastern sea, ancient Judea can never be the country of Israel restored.

Thirteenth. Our country is the land described by the prophet Isaiah *lying westward from Judea*.

"Woe to the land shadowing with wings, which is beyond the rivers of Ethiopia, that sendeth messengers by the sea, even in vessels of bulrushes, saying, Go, ye swift messengers, to a nation scattered and peeled, to a people terrible from their beginning hitherto: a nation meted out and trodden down, whose land the rivers have spoiled." Isa. xviii, 1, 2.

The word "woe" is not a malediction here, being *hoi erets* in Hebrew, a particle of hailing; and authorizes us to read, "*All hail,* thou land shadowing with wings." But where is that land? From Judea, the stand-point of the prophet, it is "beyond the rivers of Ethiopia." Where are the rivers of Ethiopia? The Nile and its tributaries. What country and what people do we find beyond the Nile from Judea? The land is a barren desert, and the wandering Bedouins the only human beings that pass through it. Then we must look for another country and another people, but in the *same direction,* for that is specific. You will find no other land or people on that line of latitude until you strike the United States of America about the coasts of Carolina. Should it be contended that Western Africa was not the ancient Ethiopia, but the country inhabited by the Cushites or children of Cush, very well; they extended eastwardly until the Ganges, the Indus, and the Burrampooter were their rivers; and beyond these from Judea you come direct to the North American continent across the Pacific. So that, in either case, "the land beyond the rivers" of modern or ancient Ethiopia from Judea is America. Its description —"a land shadowing with wings"—might refer to the geographical conformation of the new continent, for a large map of North and South America very much resembles the expanded wings of a great eagle; or it may be suggestive of the fact that it was the country shadowed or concealed from the cupidity of the nations till God was ready for its discovery. Or was it not designed as a description of a country, the national ægis of whose people should be an eagle, whose pinions should spread from shore to shore? The "swift ships" and "vessels of bulrushes" are peculiarly descriptive of our fleets of commerce, as light water-crafts of this material were anciently used upon the Nile.

This land was originally possessed by "a people hitherto terrible from the beginning." Such is a true description of the fierce and warlike aborigines who were found in this new world. "A people scattered and peeled:" broken up into numerous tribes, dispersed without order over the whole country, and wasted by continual wars, were fast waning and melting away. "Meted out and trodden down:" driven from one part of the country to another, first located in one defined territory and then in another; oppressed, maltreated, and murdered. "Whose land the rivers have spoiled:" they being the original claimants and proprietors of a country extensive in its domain and rich in its alluvial lands, through which majestic rivers are ever changing their mighty channels.

This prophetic delineation of our country can have no other meaning or application. And learned commentators, never having dreamed that America was the subject of prophecy, acknowledge as does Dr. Adam Clarke, especially, "that this is the most obscure passage in the whole book of Isaiah." Our interpretation is certainly legitimate; while the facts and the fulfillment should awaken our attention and enkindle our admiration.

Fourteenth. But the promised nationality was to be *a republic.*

"Their nobles shall be of themselves, and their governor shall proceed from the midst of them." Jer. xxx, 21. The people should be "gathered together, and appoint unto themselves one head."

Hos. i, 11. "I will restore thy judges as at the first, and thy counsellors as at the beginning." Isa. i, 26. Observe, "one head"—a chief magistrate appointed by the people—governors, judges, and counsellors, taken from the masses of the people, are particularly promised, but no king.

The political economy of ancient Israel being a theocratic republic, the promise in the passages is, that the officers necessary to constitute a republican form of government would be restored, and the elective franchise would be free, and the people would possess the sovereign right of choosing their own rulers and judges. Surely, the doctrine of the Divine right of kings finds no authority here; for the power invested in the people is entirely inconsistent with any grade of monarchy, limited or absolute.

The truth is, the fifth great commonwealth that the God of heaven was to "set up," was so utterly repugnant to monarchy, in all its forms and phases, that it should destroy it from the face of the earth. And we have every assurance that if the Almighty designed to bless a people by conferring upon them a particular form of political government, such form could not possibly be a monarchy.

A most memorable instance of the Divine disapprobation of the establishment of an earthly king among men is recorded at the coronation of the first monarch of Israel. Said Almighty God to Samuel the prophet, "*Protest solemnly* unto them, and show unto them the manner of the king that shall reign over them. He will take your sons, and appoint them for himself, for his chariots, and to be his horsemen; and some shall run before his chariots. And he will take your daughters to be confectionaries, and to be cooks, and to be bakers. And he will take your fields, and your vineyards, and your olive-yards, even the best of them, and give them to his servants. And he will take the tenth of your seed, and of your vineyards, and give them to his officers, and to his servants. And he will take your men-servants, and your maid-servants, and your goodliest young men, and your asses, and put them to work. He will take the tenth of your sheep; and ye shall be his servants. And ye shall cry out in that day because of your king, and the Lord will not hear you in that day." 1 Sam. viii, 9–18. Such is the solemn protestation of the God of heaven against an earthly monarchy; and faithfully has the history of earthly kings confirmed the truth of the Divine prediction. Then it is absolutely certain that a political government, selected and "set up" for the sons of men by Jehovah, would not be a monarchy. But this very fifth government was to be "set up" by the God of heaven; therefore the fifth government, not being in any possible case a monarchy in any grade, must be a republic.

Fifteenth and finally. The *waiting isles* of Isaiah are a sublime announcement of our great country, and its early occupation by European emigrants. "Surely, the isles shall wait for me, and the ships of Tarshish first, to bring my sons from far, their silver and their gold with them, unto the name of the Lord thy God, and to the Holy One of Israel."

Diodorus Siculus, a most reliable historian of the Augustine age, says that "the term 'isles,' in his time, primarily meant undiscovered lands supposed to exist in the Atlantic Ocean." The word "Tarshish," according to Strabo, refers to Tartessus, formerly a seaport city of that name, situated on the site where Cadiz now stands, in Old Spain, near the pillars of Hercules. And Mr. Benson, perhaps the most accurate commentator on the ancient geography of the Scriptures, says that "this opinion is now generally adopted by the learned."

With this explanation of terms, let us read the passage: "Surely, the undiscovered lands in the western sea shall wait for me, and the ships of Old

Spain shall be first to bring my sons from far, their silver and their gold with them," etc.

Here we have the fact announced, that the country spoken of had hitherto been an undiscovered country, and the reason assigned why it should have remained concealed so long—"shall wait for me"—unknown and unexplored, until God, in his supervision of the nations, was ready for its occupation. "Wait for" God, until the Reformation in Europe had neutralized the friends of civil and religious liberty: until the great principle of self-government should move the masses of the people to seek a new theatre to realize the blessings of popular freedom—wait until the facilities of intellectual and moral improvement, the invention of printing, and the freedom of the pulpit, should arise as the powerful auxiliaries of an enlightened republican nation. "And the ships of Old Spain shall be first, to bring my sons from far." And were not the ships of Spain *first* in the discovery and opening up of emigration to the New World? After being repulsed from every court in Europe to which he appealed, was not Columbus sanctioned and sustained by Ferdinand and Isabella in his expedition? "To bring my sons from far." Now, remember this passage cannot apply to the spread of the gospel, for the tidings of salvation are *sent out* to heathen lands; but here the sons of God are represented as being transported from their original homes to a newly discovered country. It cannot refer to Judea, for that was not an undiscovered country, and the ships of Spain never have brought, and never can bring, its first emigration to people it. "Their silver and their gold with them:" that they might make that land their permanent home, bringing their treasure with them. But the great motive of their emigration deserves special attention. They were to come for the privilege of worshiping God "unto the name of the Lord thy God, and to the Holy One of Israel." Our noble ancestry, driven by the storms of persecution from the Old World, sought a refuge in the New. When the minions of monarchy invaded the Southern hemisphere, it was for the sake of gold. The Portuguese in Brazil, Cortez in Mexico, and Pizarro in Peru, took possession of those countries in the names of the majesties of their respective governments. But when the Huguenots, the Quakers, and the Puritans came to America, they took possession of these lands in the name of Almighty God.

"Not as the conquerors come,
They the true-hearted came:
Not with the roll of the stirring drum,
Or the trumpet that sings of fame.

"Not as the flying come,
In silence and in fear,
They shook the depths of the desert gloom
With their hymns of lofty cheer.

"Amid the storm they sang,
And the stars heard and the sea;
And the waiting isles of promise rang
With the anthems of the free.

The ocean eagle soared
From his nest by the white wave's foam;
And the rocking pines of the forest roared,
This is your welcome home.

"What sought they thus afar?
Bright jewels of the mine?
The wealth of seas, the spoils of war?
They sought a faith's pure shrine.

"All, call it holy ground,
The spot where first they trod:
They've left unstained what there they found,
Freedom to worship God."

To review the history of our great nation is but to trace the wonderful providence of God. Look at the very men who directed and guarded the infancy of our republic; whether in the cabinet or in the camp, whether in the national council or on foreign diplomacy, "their like we shall never see again." For this very end they seemed to have been born; and they evidently believed in their Divine destination.

There was a time when darkness shrouded the breath of heaven ; not one gleam of light nor a solitary star was seen struggling through the dim distance. Congress paused under the dreadful gloom, when it was agreed to submit their cause to the arbitration of Heaven. A day of solemn fasting and prayer was proposed : instantly the resolution passed with deep emotion. The council-chamber was closed ; grave senators retired in silence, personally to engage in fervent prayer ; holy ministers of God at the altar, and pious women, with their babes pressed to their bosoms, lifted their streaming eyes to heaven ; while Washington was on his knees, when "a nation was born at once"—born on the 4th day of July, 1776.

Preserved as "an handful of corn scattered on the summit of the mountains, a little one has become a thousand, and a small one a strong nation." "It is the Lord's doings, and marvelous in our eyes ;" for, according to his promise, "the Lord has hastened it in his time."

O happy America ! O favored children of the free ! when will the great heart of thy mighty people fully know God and the salvation of his Son ! "Then Gentiles and kings shall see thy glory, and thou shalt be called by a new name, which the mouth of the Lord shall name. Thou shalt no more be termed Forsaken: neither shall thy land any more be termed Desolate: but thou shalt be called Hephzi-bah, and thy land Beulah: for the Lord delighteth in thee." Then shall thy glory continue; for "Thy sun shall no more go down, neither shall thy moon withdraw itself; for the Lord shall be thine everlasting light, and the days of thy mourning shall be ended."

The Battle of Armageddon,

OR

THE WORLD'S LAST CONFLICT BETWEEN CIVIL AND RELIGIOUS LIBERTY ON THE ONE SIDE, AND POLITICAL AND ECCLESIASTICAL DESPOTISM ON THE OTHER.

THE voice of the prophetic Scriptures frequently and fully announces the warfare of the world. Preparation for ages has anticipated the struggle; while the clangor of its trumpets is almost heard marshaling its millions to the charge.

It is as true as destiny; and the gathering storm is rising. In the volume of inspiration it is termed, "The Battle of Gog," "The Battle of Armageddon," and "The Battle of that great day of God Almighty."

It is symbolized by Daniel in the smiting of the monarchical image by the mountain-stone; by the casting down of the thrones before the Ancient of days; by the destruction of the willful king upon the mountains of Israel, when he shall "plant the tabernacles of his palace between the two seas." It is Michael and his angels warring with the dragon and his angels; it is the conquest won by the man on a white horse, who was "crowned with many crowns;" it is the taking of "the beast and the false prophet;" it is the reaping the harvest of the world and the gathering of the vintage of the earth. It is literally described by Ezekiel, when the chief prince of Meshech, Gomer, Tubal, and Magog, with the multitudinous hosts from Persia, Ethiopia, and Libya, invades "the land of unwalled villages." It is the immense armament described by Joel when he exclaims, "Multitudes! multitudes in the valley of decision!" It is described by the Saviour to be "a time of trouble such as never shall be till that day." It is the "gathering together of the kings and nations of the earth to the battle of that great day of God Almighty."

Such, my countrymen, are some of the unquestionable and sublime allusions in the many, very many Divine declarations that announce the grand and terrible catastrophe—declarations that the clearest acumen and most direct philosophy of language must legitimately apply to the rapidly approaching tempest.

Nevertheless, like all other truths of the inspired volume, however overwhelming the sublimity of the theme, no violence is offered to reason, nor unnecessary embargo imposed upon the faith of mortals.

What subject could possibly enlist a world in arms, if it be not the principle of civil and religious liberty? All other questions, however vital and important, are but local in their influence, and the weightiest results must necessarily be sectional. But the principle of popular freedom is capable of universal diffusion, and must ultimately be commensurate with the nations of the earth. It lies at the foundation of our being, and forms the very texture and fabric of human nature: nay, the very law of our great Creator, and every specification growing out of that law, bear directly upon this twofold principle. To love God and our neighbor plainly indicates the foundation of all true order in the governmental codes of the earth. Freedom to worship God, and equitable reciprocities amongst our fellow-creatures: wherever these first and great commandments are disregarded by the governments on earth, monarchy, absolutism, or anarchy is found to exist; and this form of government being unfriendly to the free worship of the true God, and a usurpation of the prerogatives of a people to govern themselves, always has been, and ever will be, an uncompromising enemy to civil and religious liberty, until it is annihilated from the nations of the earth.

True, both principles are aggressive, and must continue to enlarge their bounds until a final collision must exterminate the one or the other.

The outbreaks in ages past were only occasional or accidental; still, even in those times monarchy always reconnoitred with a sleepless vigilance every demonstration of popular freedom; and the genius of Republicanism has ever been prompt to prove its utter, uncompromising hostility to monarchy. But in those ages the world was too far apart, the knowledge of the nations too limited, and their contact with one another so seldom, that they seemed to live in comparative indifference to one another. But now, since intellectual and moral light is reaching every shore; commerce spreading every where; the formal representatives of all nations at the world's fairs, in London, New York, and Paris; since the wonderful discoveries of gold in California and Australia, bringing the nations together; and since the facilities for travel by land and by sea, and the intercommunication of the magnetic telegraph—the world has come into such immediate proximity, the great issue must come off. The hostile forms of government are now clearly defined and well understood; and the two geniuses, like two Cæsars, cannot live in the same world together much longer. For if Republicanism be a failure, it will be overthrown; and if Absolutism be offensive to God, and an outrage upon the people, its days are destined to be numbered.

The truth, as announced in the Bible, of the coming conflict, has always been received in the Church, because too obvious to be questioned. Both Jews and Christians maintain it as a subject of Divine revelation: but as they have almost invariably misapplied the passages that foretold a great nationality, by referring them to the Jews, it necessarily led them to lay the scene of the last great battle in the land of Palestine. That the scattered Jews would return to Judea, and the nations and kingdoms of the earth would send an armament of millions to crush out a handful of unambitious people, whom the clemency of Christian countries favored in their return—how perfectly ridiculous! Were all the Jews on earth restored to the small territory of Palestine, what temptation or provocation could they offer to arouse the allied armies of earth to invade them?

No, my countrymen, it is not ancient Jewry that will witness this invasion. There is another Israel, the Israel of America, that has given monarchy more disquietude than ancient Israel ever did in all its glory. And here alone monarchy will find a foeman worthy of its steel, and the only nation on the globe that can measure arms with kings.

Twice in the very infancy of our nation's history the proudest empire on the face of the earth had to pay an involuntary obeisance to the chivalry of our army. But now that the young eaglet is fully fledged, and cleaves the heights of heaven, it might be indiscreet to provoke the glance of his eye or the thunder of his pinions. So at least we think.

We shall first notice the preparatory movements that will finally marshal the allied hosts to battle:

"And the sixth angel poured out his vial upon the great river Euphrates; and the water thereof was dried up, that the way of the kings of the east might be prepared. And I saw three unclean spirits like frogs come out of the mouth of the dragon, and out of the mouth of the beast, and out of the mouth of the false prophet. For they are the spirits of devils, working miracles, which go forth unto the kings of the earth and of the whole world, to gather them to the battle of that great day of God Almighty. . . And he gathered them together into a place called in the Hebrew tongue Armageddon."

Now, observe, whatever may be the meaning of the sublime events mentioned in the foregoing passage, they must relate to the preparatory measures that bring on the battle of that great day.

Let us, then, examine the quotation by the most reliable rules of interpretation. A "*river*" in the symbolic prophecies, according to the admission of the best commentators, symbolizes a national commotion. Then, "the great river Euphrates," that swept by encient Babylon, must represent a great commotion or revolution among the nations; but this scene is laid under the sixth vial, which is now acknowledged to embrace the beginning of the present century. Well, when was there ever a greater commotion among the nations than the revolutionary upheavings of the people under the genius of the great Napoleon? But "the waters of that river were dried up." This was done at the battle of Waterloo. "That the way of the kings of the east might be prepared." During the storm that was raging throughout Europe under Bonaparte, the allied monarchs that were united to overthrow him found it very inconvenient to act in concert; but immediately after Napoleon was banished to a distant island, there was an assemblage of the principal monarchs: Russia, Prussia, Austria, and England. Though the King of England could not be there in person—for the old man was crazy—yet his regent was there, and represented him in that conference, that was called "*The Triple Alliance.*" This name may have been given to this conclave of kings from the three principal monarchs in attendance. But this "triple alliance" has a stronger claim to its *threefold* character from the *three doctrines*, asserted, signed, and sealed by this convention of sovereigns. There were precisely *three doctrines* or principles: *Absolutism*, *Church Supremacy*, and *Legitimacy*, or the *Divine right of kings*. How perfectly fulfilled the prophecy! "*And I saw three unclean spirits* like frogs come out of the mouth of the dragon, and out of the mouth of the beast, and out of the mouth of the false prophet. These are the spirits of devils." The three dogmas are here pronounced to be the spirits or doctrines of devils. All doctrines are the doctrines of devils that are opposed by Divine revelation; but Absolutism, Church Supremacy, and Divine right of kings, are opposed by the word of God; consequently, the three doctrines of the "Triple Alliance" are the doctrines of devils, and specifically fulfill the prophecy. "Which go forth unto the kings of the earth and of the whole world, to gather them together to the battle of that great day of God Almighty." These foul principles represented by *unclean frogs* will summon around the thrones of monarchies the dupes of despotism, and enlist and muster into service the countless legions that shall compose that fearful armament. "And he gathered them together into a place called in the Hebrew tongue Armageddon." On that last great battle-field, the doctrines of the Triple Alliance, with the hosts of their deluded defenders, shall perish for ever.

We now notice some of the symbols of that final engagement, the war itself.

"Forasmuch as thou sawest that the stone was cut out of the mountain without hands, and that it brake in pieces the iron, the brass, the clay, the silver, and the gold; the great God hath made known to the king what shall come to pass hereafter: and the dream is certain, and the interpretation thereof sure."

The four great successive monarchies on earth, as seen in the dream of Nebuchadnezzar, we have shown in our former address to be represented by the metals composing the great image. From the first or golden headed kingdom, the whole of monarchy, to its final overthrow, was represented; for after the annihilation of this image, not the smallest principle or fragment should remain. "Then was the iron, the clay, the brass, the silver, and the gold, broken to pieces together, and became like the chaff of the summer threshing-floors; and the wind carried them away, that no place was found for them." But how are we to understand all these great monarchies to be *destroyed at once*, "broken to pieces together," unless we understand that before that image is smitten by the stone, there must be a reconstruction of all the principles and powers, glory and grandeur, weakness and wickedness, embodied in the corporate image, and represented by the different metals. Such an accumulation of all the principles of monarchy, in some colossal giant of autocracy, must appear in huge embodiment: "the form thereof," like its symbol, will be "terrible." Now, as we have plainly proved that the stone or fifth kingdom that destroys the image is a different kind of government altogether from monarchy, and hostile to it, that fifth government must be a great Republic. In truth, as monarchy restored is seen in the image, Israel, or a providential Republic, must be restored also, in order to the destruction of monarchy.

Let those divines attend who suppose that Christianity is " the stone cut out of the mountain without hands." Which of the four great empires did Christianity destroy? The truth is, the Assyrian, the Medo-Persian, and the Macedonian kingdoms had passed away long before Christianity was born. And as for Rome, certainly no good Christian would ever dream that the barbarian hordes from the North who overran the Roman Empire were either good or bad Christians.

From this symbol we are clearly taught:

First. That the whole of monarchy, from the Assyrian down to its utter destruction, is represented in the dream.

Second. That a political government, unconnected with, different from, and hostile to monarchy, would providentially arise in the divided age of the Roman Empire.

Third. That this fifth or stone government would destroy the last vestige of monarchy from the face of the earth.

Fourth. That the destruction of monarchy will be effected by military power. The strong language employed to describe the destruction of the metallic image cannot refer to the gentle and inoffensive religion of Christ. The power of moral suasion, by gradual influence, will change the heart and manners of men. But to overthrow at one single blow a vast political organization, combining millions of subjects, the custom of ages, and the wealth of nations, and that, too by the mild and gentle genius of a religion whose great Author was meek and lonely, and whose kingdom was not of this world, is out of the question. The very terms used to describe the destruction of the Macedonian Empire by the Roman are also employed to show the annihilation of all the empires by the stone. Now, the conquests made by Rome were effected by the prowess of her arms: none will deny this. If, therefore, Rome herself and the balance of the kingdoms are to be destroyed, it must be by military power also.

The destruction effected by this fearful power is complete, for the image is broken and reduced to infinitesimal atoms: it is scattered to the winds, like chaff from the summer's threshing-floors.

As this conflict puts a final end to all earthly

monarchy, and as all political governments are either autocratic or democratic, and as the fifth government is to "become a great mountain and fill the whole world," the conclusion is forced upon us that one of the grand missions of the providential Republic of America is the final overthrow of monarchy and the extension of the principles of popular freedom over the whole world.

The vision of Daniel the prophet was a corroboration of the dream of Nebuchadnezzar the king. The four beasts of Daniel answer to the four metals of the image. The ten horns on the head of the fourth beast answer to the ten toes on the feet of the image. The little horn having eyes, that arose on the head of the last beast, and amongst the other horns, symbolized an ecclesiastical connection with the state, and answers to the union of the clay and iron in the feet. The rise of the Ancient upon a chariot throne symbolizes a pure political government, combining the principles of a confederated republic, such as was the "ancient" form of government given to the Jews, and answers to the stone "cut out of the mountain without hands." The casting down of the thrones before the Ancient answers to the smiting of the monarchical image by the stone. The coming of "one like to the

Son of man to the Ancient," and the "dominion given to the people of the saints," answer to the stone becoming "a great mountain and filling the whole earth;" and both symbolize the universal spread of civil and religious liberty, until the millennial glory of Christ shall cover the earth as the waters cover the seas.

The vision is indeed a sublime one; and the inexpressible grandeur of the scene has inclined most men to suppose that "the Ancient of days" was the Almighty Father. But how can this be? For this is evidently a judgment-scene of the doom of monarchy; for this alone, it seems, the judgment did sit and "the thrones were cast down." But "the Father judgeth no man." God the Father is in no place in the Scriptures represented by a human form. Besides, the Almighty is not the "Ancient of days:" he is the Ancient of eternity. And the term "days" is evidently used in this passage to let men understand that the vision refers to time, and its scenes are to be transacted on earth. Nor can the "Ancient" refer to the Son of man, for it is written in the vision that "one like unto the Son of man came to the Ancient" afterwards.

"And there was war in heaven: Michael and his

angels fought against the dragon; and the dragon fought and his angels, and prevailed not; neither was their place found any more in heaven. And the great dragon was cast out." Rev. xii, 7, 8.

This passage is another symbolic announcement of the grand conflict. The contending armies, the battle-scene and its results, are respectively mentioned.

"A dragon," being fabulous, is necessarily a symbol; for, although the word has been applied first to one beast and then to another, there is no certainty if it had any identical original. But the tyrants of the ancient kingdoms were called *dragons:* the despots of Egypt in particular were denominated thus. The Scriptures being then their own interpreter, a dragon is the symbol of political despotism. Now, as the one part is symbolic, the other must be also. Then "Michael" is not, in this case, a literal angel, but stands as the representative of a power opposed to autocracy. That power can only be the genius of popular freedom. Perfectly agreeable to this definition is the character drawn of this same Michael in the Book of Daniel. He is there called "Michael the great prince, that standeth for the children of thy people:" that is, he is the illustration and exponent of the genius of liberty or the sovereignty of the people. The term "heaven" in the passage is also symbolic, and means, when used in the Apocalypse, the *place of the Church,* as the term "earth," when employed under the same circumstances, refers to the seat of the old Roman Empire. As for "war in heaven," the place of future blessedness, no dragon or war will ever be known there; for "there the wicked cease to trouble, and the weary are at rest."

Then the war which is to take place between Michael and his angels on the one side, and the dragon and his angels on the other, must foretell the final battle that must inevitably occur between civil and religious liberty and its armies and monarchy and its armies, which, according to the prediction, closes with the glorious triumph of the former over the ruin and annihilation of the latter.

"Michael, the great prince that standeth for thy people," must then, in the book of Revelation, be understood as the symbolic embodiment of popular sovereignty. But, my countrymen, if any one man that ever lived on earth is entitled to be called Michael, the great prince that standeth for the people, it is George Washington, the friend of liberty, and the father of his country.

"And I saw heaven opened, and behold a white horse; and he that sat upon him, . . and in righteousness he doth judge and make war. His eyes were as a flame of fire, and on his head were many crowns. . . And I saw the beast, and the kings of the earth, and their armies, gathered together to make war against him that sat on the horse, and against his army. And the beast was taken, and with him the false prophet. . . And the remnant were slain with the sword of him that sat upon the horse." Rev. xix.

From the best annotators of prophecy, the following is the true and legitimate interpretation of the terms employed:

First. A "horse" is a symbol of some form of religion; consequently, a "white horse" must represent a pure and divinely authorized religion.

Second. A "man" symbolizes a political government.

Third. "Crowns" represent sovereignties: "many crowns upon his head"—many State sovereignties united in one political union or confederation. When this same symbolic personage appeared as "the man-child," the number of States represented by the stars was *twelve*, then *thirteen;* but now, since the infant "is one hundred years old" at the commencement of the great war, he appears on the battle-field, "crowned with many crowns"—many more States in the confederacy than at the beginning.

Then, we behold in this vision of St. John a political government embracing a confederation of many State sovereignties, acknowledging and confiding in one true and divinely sanctioned religion.

That the United States of America answers to this picture, our very national "E PLURIBUS UNUM" declares.

Here again we behold the forces of monarchy mustered to give battle to a free confederated Republic that sanctions the only true religion. "For the beast, and the kings of the earth, and their armies, gathered together to make war against him that sat upon the horse, and against his army." The taking of the beast, and the false prophet, and the kings of the earth, and their armies, and the slaying of the remnant by the sword of him that sat upon the horse, foretell the overthrow and utter destruction of the allied armies of monarchy, by an enlightened confederated Republic in one great decisive battle.

The symbols are so numerous, the imagery so perfectly descriptive of each respective scene, and the correspondence of each member so wonderfully adapted to complete the symmetry of the whole, we are bound to behold their fulfillment in the rise and growing grandeur of a great consolidated Republic on the one hand, and the reconstruction of the autocracy of antiquity in some vast empire on the other. These two colossal powers will meet in a last decisive struggle.

So far as the historic panorama has disclosed the subject, the accumulating coincidences are remarkably true, and on a sublime scale. These two great powers are the United States of America and the monarchy of Russia, both widely extending the magnitude of their greatness; so that, in the present state of affairs, a perfect coincidence of facts answers a perfect description of prophecy. We look to the future for the finale of these startling wonders, to be fulfilled in a conflict that will enlist all nations, stir the world with commotion, and drench the earth with blood.

We now call your attention to a literal and most graphic description of the last conflict.

Ezekiel the priest, the son of Buzi, while amongst the captives by the river Chebor, saw the heavens open, and had visions of God.

In the thirty-eighth and thirty-ninth chapters of

his prophecy, he gives us a full, literal, and detailed description of this battle; yet it is most astonishing that although this account is plain, presenting in the *concrete* and the *minutiæ* the whole subject, commentators in the old continent declare that it is the most mysterious and perplexing portion of all Ezekiel's writings. Did it not appear uncharitable, we would be led to suppose that the only difficulty in the case was the doom of monarchy, so plainly announced, that a legitimate comment of its true meaning might not be favorably received by the fawning friends of the political systems of the old world. But God "has magnified his word above all his name,"

> "And what his mouth in truth hath said,
> His own almighty hand will do."

The invading army, and the multitudinous hosts of its allies, are particularly mentioned by their appropriate names and the countries they represent; the geographical location and territorial description of the land to be invaded; the character of its inhabitants, their quietude and prosperity; the unprovoked nature of the attack: the suicidal policy of the invasion, as declared by the almighty; the solicitude of the invaded people to know the cause of the campaign; the universal agitation and commotion of the whole people so invaded; the battle-field; the Divine interposition in behalf of the invaded; the unbroken unanimity of all the States and Territories in resisting the foe; the overwhelming triumph over monarchy; the immensity of the armament, as seen in the sepulture of the slain and the wrecks of battle; the simultaneous insurrection of the subjects of monarchy at home; the glorious results of the contest; the annihilation of despotism, and the world-wide extension of popular free dom—all, all are announced in the programme of the prophet.

First, then, let us know *who leads this invasion?*

"Son of man, set thy face against Gog, the land of Magog, the chief prince of Meshech and Tubal, and prophesy against him, and say, Thus saith the Lord God: Behold, I am against thee, O Gog, the chief prince of Meshech and Tubal: and I will turn thee back, and put hooks into thy jaws, and I will bring thee forth, and all thine army, horses and horsemen, all of them clothed with all sorts of armor, even a great company with bucklers and shields, all of them handling swords: Persia, Ethiopia, and Libya with them; all of them with shield and helmet: Gomer, and all his bands, the house of Togarmah of the north quarters, and all his bands: and many people with thee."

Now, whosoever these people may be, "the chief prince," or great leading sovereignty of the invasion is found among them. Hence this direct address of the Almighty to that prince. And that this prince is the headship of the alliance is evident from God's personal message to him: "Be thou prepared, and prepare for thyself, thou, and all thy company that are assembled unto thee, and be thou a guard unto them." Here, then is the leading power marked out in the prophecy, to which the allied armies will be assembled.

This overwhelming power we shall demonstrate to be Russia.

The very names of the ancient patriarchs of the Russian dominions determine their location and nationality.

"Gog" signifies a prince or head of many countries.

"Magog, Gomer, Meshech, and Tubal," are four of the seven sons of Japtheth. (See Genesis x; 1 Chron. i.)

These patriarchs, according to Calmet, Brown, Bochart, and others, settled within the bounds of what is now the Russian dominions.

"Magog," says Josephus, "founded the Magogue, whom the Greeks call Sythee." Now, these Scythee are the Scythians who form almost one-fourth of Russian population. They extended from Hungary, Transylvania, and Wallachia, on the west, to the River Dan on the east. The Russian territory of this people embraces a large portion both of Europe and Asia.

"Meshech," the sixth son of Japheth, settled in the north-eastern portion of Asia Minor. His posterity extended from the shores of the Euxine Sea along to the south of Caucasus. He was the father of the Rossi and Moschi, who dispersed their colonies over a vast portion of Russian territory. And their names are preserved in the names of Russians and Muscovites to this day. The Septuagint version of the Old Testament renders the term Meshech by the words Mosch and Rosch; while Moscovy is a common name of Russia, and the city of Moscow is one of their principal cities.

"Tubal," or Tobal, the fifth son of Japheth, settled beyond the Caspian and Black Seas in the eastern possessions of Russia, embracing a very large portion of those dominions. The name of this patriarch is still preserved in the river Tobal, which waters an immense tract of Russian territory; and the city of Tobalski in Russia is still a monument to this son of Japheth.

From all which, it is certain that, as Magog, Meshech, and Tubal compose the present possessions of Russia, the sovereignty of that empire is the chief prince addressed in the prophetic message.

"Gomer, and all his bands; the house of Togarmah of the north quarters, and all his bands, and many people with thee."

"Gomer," another son of Japheth, settled farther down westward in Europe; and has left his name entailed in Hungary, in a city and country both known to this day as the city and country of Gomer.

"Togarmah," the son of Gomer, according to Cicero and Strabo, not only peopled a large portion of Western Europe, but sent settlements into Turcomania and Scythia in Russia.

Russia, then, according to the Scriptures, is the headship or leading power around which the multitudinous armies of allied monarchy shall be gathered together.

"Persia, Ethiopia, and Libya with them; all of them with shield and helmet."

Persia here represents the swarming hosts from the Asiatic possessions; Ethiopia and Libya, the armies from Africa.

"Thou shalt ascend and come like a storm, thou shalt be like a cloud to cover the land, thou, and all thy bands, and many people with thee."

The invasion is here announced by an armament such as the world never saw. For the millions that are to assemble under Gog or Russia embrace nearly all of Europe, as well as a large portion of Asia and Africa. This army is drafted from three continents to invade a fourth. It rises dismal as a cloud, and dreadful as a storm.

We must look to Russia, then, as the colossal giant of reconstructed monarchy, embodying the whole of autocracy in the last grand organization —embracing all the principles foreshadowed in the metallic symbol of the vision "whose brightness was excellent, and the form thereof terrible." In fact, the Emperor of all the Russias still bears the royal cognomen of the golden-headed monarchs of ancient Babylon. Who is the present Emperor of Russia? Alexander *the Czar*. And who are found among the monarchs of Assyria? Nobonazar, Nebuchadnezzar, and Belshazzar. These were not accidental terminations of their respective names, but were doubtless terms of Assyrian royalty. So also the Roman *Cæsars*, which scarcely vary from the true pronunciation of the *czars*. We behold in Russia the original trunk of autocracy. In the time of Catharine, she arose in august magnitude, and entered into the European state system about the time of the rise of our great country. We see rising on the one hand and on the other, the two great powers that represent respectively their opposing principles of government that will come in collision in the last dreadful fray.

The United States of America, young and vigorous, arising in the Northern temperate zone, with untold resources, extending its borders from sea to sea, and from the lakes in the North to Heaven only knows how far South—she is the enlightened and uncompromising representative of popular freedom. And there is Russia in gigantic proportions, arising also in the Northern temperate zone, with her million of warriors, now occupying one-seventh of earth's *terra-firma*, stretching from the Black Sea to the Arctic Ocean, and from the Baltic on the West, till her Cossacks almost hear the British drums beat in farther India. And she is the representative of absolutism.

These ascending powers, like two towering clouds culminating in the heavens, surcharged with electric ruin, will shock the world with their collision, and bathe the world in blood.

But allied with Russia will be the teeming myriads from all the empires on earth except France—belle France. France will be with us in the end, as she was with us in the beginning.* We feel warranted for this position. Commentators agree, that when the state system in Europe is represented in the Apocalypse by the celestial bodies, France is appropriately denominated "*the sun*," not only from its vivacity and brilliancy, but especially from its central position to the rest of Europe. "And I saw an angel standing in the sun; and he cried with a loud voice, saying to all the fowls that fly in the midst of heaven, Come, and gather yourselves together unto the supper of the great God, that ye may eat the flesh of kings," etc. Rev. xix. This angel, must, therefore, represent the genius of France, rejoicing over the downfall of monarchy; consequently, will be with America in the final struggle. A strong undercurrent for civil and religious liberty has frequently

* In delivering the above sentence in the Hall of Representatives, the assembly turned their attention to a large life-like portrait of Lafayette, hanging on the walls of the Capitol, opposite that of Washington. We had not observed Lafayette's portrait till that moment, as it was on our left. The expression, "France will be with us in the end, as she was with us in the beginning," seemed to make a profound sensation, as they saw no other nation on the canvas but France and America. The coincidence was impressive upon our own mind as it evidently was with the audience.

risen to the surface in the French nation; and under its power she will break her alliance with monarchy, and join the standard of liberty against the despotisms of the world.

But England, true to her proud autocracy, will die for the Divine right of kings. Her policy will not be influenced by language, religion, nor blood; but in the final onset she will join the crusade against America.

When was she ever known to favor an oppressed people attempting to throw off the yoke of despotism? Look at her tender mercies toward her own children when struggling in the war of Independence. See how she let loose "the horrible hell-hounds of savage cruelty," when she turned the bloody Indian, with tomahawk and scalping-knife, upon helpless women and children; and even rewarded the savage furies with a *pound sterling* for every scalp that was taken, whether from the poor old man, the defenceless mother, or the sucking babe. Look at her cruelties with her pagan slaves in India. Even now, who can look to China without emotion? Behold how she gloated over ill-fated Hungary. When the friends of freedom were immolated in crowds by Austrian despots—when delicate females were cowhided in the streets by the incarnate fiend Haynau—England, by a nod, could have suppressed the whole. Talk of English sympathy for the children of Africa in America! What consummate hypocrisy! when, at the same time, thousands of her own pauper people are suffered to live like beasts, or rather to die like dogs, if not confined for long years in her mines, without seeing the light of day, but working in traces like mules, on all-fours, to fatten the fortunes of English aristocracy. Do you doubt the picture? it is drawn by an official report to Parliament. Alas, let Ireland, from centuries of miserable oppression, say what heart has England to aid the friends of freedom against the despotism of usurpation.

No: England will be allied with Russia. Her *policy, not her love,* may sustain amicable relations while it suits her, but no longer. But her glory is departing. She has gambled with the world till she has lost the sword. When the Empress of the British Isles visited the tomb of Napoleon, to pay honor to the ashes of the dead whom her own government had outlawed while living, it was then England's waning renown was seen in the rising splendors of the French nation. "Ichabod" is already written on the palaces of her power. Self-preservation will conglomerate the autocratic powers of the Old World in one stupendous attack upon that nation whose republican principles and brilliant example have already disquieted the repose of princes, and made each royal diadem a crown of thorns.

"Thus saith the Lord God: it shall also come to pass, that at the same time shall things come into thy mind, and thou shalt think an evil thought. Thou shalt say, I will go up to the land of unwalled villages: I will go to them that are at rest, that dwell safely, all of them dwelling without walls, and having neither bars nor gates. To take a spoil, and to take a prey; to turn thine hand upon the desolate places that are now inhabited, and upon the people that are gathered out of the nations, which have gotten cattle and goods, that dwell in the midst of the land." Ezek. xxxviii. The Almighty pronounces the invasion impolitic—that the expedition was from "an evil thought;" and what was foreseen and foretold to be planned in weakness or wickedness, will, by its disastrous realization, confirm the truth of the Divine declaration

The land to be invaded is, in the foregoing quotation, a literal and true description of the United

States, and can apply to no other country or people under heaven. A country highly elevated—the land once a wilderness or desolate, but now inhabited—a "land of unwalled villages"—a "people gathered out of the nations"—a people "that dwell safely"—proprietors of the country, dwelling at rest—a people prosperous in their fortunes, having "gotten cattle and goods, dwelling in the midst of the land." It is the same country described by the prophet "between the two seas;" and by Daniel, when, after describing the conquests of "the willful king of the North," (Russia,) in carrying his victorious armies "into the glorious land," (Palestine,) he hears tidings from the North and from the East which trouble him, and he "comes in great wrath" away from Palestine, and plants the tabernacles of his palaces "in the glorious holy mountain." Upon this high country he falls, and is "broken without hands." This glorious mountain cannot be Judea, for the invader has just returned from Judea to "go up to the land of unwalled villages."

"After many days thou shalt be visited: in the latter years thou shalt come unto the land that is gathered out of many people. . . I will bring thee forth, and all thine army, horses and horsemen, all of them clothed with all sorts of armor, even a great company with bucklers and shields, all of them handling swords." Observe, the scene of this battle is laid "in the latter years," which must correspond with the conflict which is yet to come; the expression being always understood in prophecy to refer to the thrilling times immediately preceding the millennium. The diversity of the implements of battle indicates the many nationalities enrolled for battle. Perhaps "horses and horsemen" peculiarly refer to the resources of Russia, who boasts that she can bring a million men into the field.

The battle-field—the Valley of the Mississippi: "And it shall come to pass in that day, that I will give unto Gog a place there of graves in Israel, the valley of the passengers on the east of the sea." Ezek. xxxix, 11.

The philosophy of our language settles the location. When two things of the same class are spoken of in the same sentence, it is according to rhetoric, in referring to the greater of the two, simply to use the definite article "the." As the prophet had referred to both seas, the eastern and the great western, now it was proper simply to say "the sea;" that is, the *Pacific*, because it is the greater. This valley lies on the east of the Pacific, then, which is precisely the relative position of the Valley of the Mississippi. But this valley east of the Mississippi is "the valley of passengers."

How justly entitled to this appellation is our great Valley, more peculiarly so than any valley in the known world! See the thousands of vessels that convey tens of thousands of passengers on more than fifty thousand miles of the Father of Waters and its navigable tributaries! look at the immense trains of people that daily traverse this valley in railroad cars, while caravan after caravan of emigrants are, and have been for years, pressing to the great West to dwell in all our vast new States and Territories—and their number increases by swarming thousands! The Valley of the Mississippi, then, on the east of the sea, is "the valley of passengers," and this is the battle-field of that last great conflict; for "there," says God, "will I give to Gog, and to the many people that are with them, a place of graves." Joel lays the scene of this startling and sublime event also in a valley: "Multitudes! multitudes in the valley of decision!"

The excitement and commotion amongst our own people will be overwhelming and universal. "In that day there shall be a great shaking in the land of Israel, so that the fishes of the sea, and the fowls of heaven, and the beasts of the field, and all creeping things that creep upon the earth, and all the men that are upon the face of the earth, shall shake at my presence, and the mountains shall be thrown down, and the steep places shall fall, and every wall shall fall to the ground."

A time, indeed, of great consternation and trouble, such as has never been since the world began!

But firm and unbroken in the dreadful shock, our confederated Republic will remain an undivided unit. For, says God, "I will call for a sword throughout all my mountains." Every State and Territory will be in the field. Our glorious Union, then, from a Divine promise, shall never dissolve. No storm-cloud in the North, or volcanic eruption in the South, will ever divide our great country. Our noble vessel, with her live-oak timbers, will reel and quiver in the dreadful squall, but she will never founder! A child of Providence, born in the tempest and cradled in the storm, was early disciplined for the august destiny that awaits it:

> "A union of lakes, and a union of lands,
> A union no power shall sever;
> A union of hearts, and a union of hands,
> And the American Union for ever!"

In the darkness of that dreadful day, when the heavens are hung with the clouds of war, and the earth vibrates with the peals of battle; when the face of the valiant is pale, and the heart of the brave is troubled; while storms portentous of annihilation howl around like the wailings of the damned—"all these are but the beginning of sorrow:" "for there shall be great tribulation, such as was not since the beginning of the world to this time, no, nor ever shall be."

It will be then, my countrymen, and not till then, that the heart of our great people will begin to understand the immediate presence of Almighty God, and the supervision of his providence in the rise, preservation, and destiny of our glorious Republic. "So will I make my holy name known in the midst of my people Israel; and I will not let them pollute my holy name any more." Ezek. xxxix.

In the universal calamity of those troublous times, we will be impelled to call upon Jehovah; and nothing can so effectually reveal the Divine presence and power as a whole nation looking to Heaven for help. To realize our dependence on Almighty God, and fully to know and appreciate the supervision of his hand, is doubtless one of the wise and gracious designs for the stormy ordeal through which we will pass. For in the very midnight of our troubles, Heaven will appear to our rescue. "It shall come to pass at the same time, when Gog shall come against the land of Israel, saith the Lord God, that my fury shall come up in my face. . . I will put hooks in thy jaws, and turn thee back. . . I will call for a sword against him throughout all my mountains. . . And I will plead against him with pestilence and with blood; and I will rain upon him, and upon his bands, and upon the many people that are with him, an overflowing rain, and great hailstones, fire, and brimstone. Thus will I magnify myself, and sanctify myself; and I will be known in the eyes of many nations, and they shall know that I am the Lord. . . And I will smite thy bow out of thy left hand, and will cause thine arrows to fall out of thy right hand. Thou shalt fall upon the mountains of Israel, thou, and all thy bands, and the people that is with thee: I will give thee unto the ravenous birds of every sort, and to the beasts of the field, to be devoured. Thou shalt fall upon the open field: for I have spoken it, saith the Lord God." Ezek. xxxix.

A similar description, with the same sublime imagery, of this battle of the great day of God Almighty will be found in the Revelation of John the evangelist. Both accounts close with the deep-toned period: "Behold, it is done, saith the Lord God." How immense that army!—doubtless many times greater than the forces with which Xerxes crossed the Hellespont into Greece; and he led two millions six hundred thousand warriors, besides as many more sutlers and followers of the camp. How wide and dreadful the carnage! This we learn from the *seven months* occupied in burying the dead, for the victors were employed all that time in the rites of sepulture; and then the wreck of battle left implements enough to be used as fuel for *seven years!*

At the very time of the overthrow of Monarchy in the field, a revolutionary "fire breaks out in the land of Magog" and in the isles of the sea: the friends of freedom at home in Russia and Great Britain strike for liberty, and the work is done.

So closes the conflict of the world. Now pæans of gladness ring through the earth, while emancipated millions join the general joy. "And I heard as it were the voice of a great multitude, and as the voice of many waters, and as the voice of mighty thunderings, saying, Alleluia: for the Lord God omnipotent reigneth."

Henceforth, "nations shall learn war no more."

Confederated Republics, under the counsel and example of the United States, will arise in the former "habitations of dragons," and the "deserts" of cruelty "shall rejoice and blossom as the rose." And, like an elder brother, our Republic will kindly instruct them in the principles of popular freedom. Now dawns that glorious day so often referred to in the Holy Scriptures—the millennium morning. Talk of converting the nations of the earth to God while monarchy lasts! What a mistake! Never can the Prince of Peace hold universal sway upon earth until the last vestige of earthly royalty is destroyed for ever. But after the casting down of the thrones, the smiting of the great image, the taking of the beast and the false prophet, the reaping of the vintage and harvest of the earth, the overthrow of the dragon and his armies, the fall of the willful king, and the slaughter of the armies of Gog at the battle of the great day of God Almighty, that bright day shall begin, long the theme of so many promises to the good and true of every age, the hallowed hope of the Christian Church, and the song that made Judah's sacred mountains shake with expectant joy. The cloudless splendor from "a new heaven" will beam upon the inhabitants of "a new earth" in that happy millennium—a thousand years—when there will be but one kind of civil government known, and that will be Republicanism, and but one religion known, and that will be Christianity. Not that every man will be a holy man, for the final judgment will come when wise and foolish virgins, the righteous and the wicked, will both be upon earth; but a long circle of ages called the millennium—a certain given for an indefinite number of years—in which the means for the elevation of the world will be multiplied, commerce and trade, agriculture and manufactures, science and art, will extend, the gospel of the Son of God have universal welcome among the nations of the earth, and "nations learn war no more." Then will the apocalyptic angel, having the everlasting gospel to preach to every nation and people and tongue, sweep the breath of heaven, and as his silvery pinions of light shave the level horizon, every island and continent shall bow obsequious to his message: "Fear God, and give glory to him; and worship him that made heaven and earth, and the sea, and the fountains of waters."

Then shall righteousness and peace among the nations walk, Messiah reign,

"And earth keep jubilee a thousand years."

www.ingramcontent.com/pod-product-compliance
Lightning Source LLC
LaVergne TN
LVHW021424110826
845150LV00007B/2078

* 9 7 8 1 4 2 5 5 0 7 7 3 2 *